COMBINATION OVEN COOKERY

COMBINATION OVEN COOKERY

Caroline Stevens and Deborah Robb

GRUB STREET LONDON

Published by
Grub Street
Golden House
28–31 Great Pulteney St
London W1

Copyright © 1987 Grub Street, London
Text Copyright © Caroline Stevens and Deborah
Robb
Design Copyright © Grub Street, London
Photographs by Paul Grater

Food prepared and styled for photography by
Caroline Stevens and Deborah Robb
Illustrations by Claire Wright

Stevens, Caroline
    Combination oven cooking.
    1. Cookery
    I. Title II. Robb, Deborah
    641.5′88   TX717

    ISBN 0–948817–08–9
    ISBN 0–948817–09–7 Pbk

Computerset by Chapterhouse, The Cloisters,
Formby
Printed and bound in Great Britain by
R J Acford, Chichester

*We would like to dedicate this book to our families
and friends who have helped us sample the recipes
that now appear in these pages. To Fran, who has
typed furiously, and to the staff of the Kitchen Design
Centre, Colchester for their support. Thanks also to
Bosch and Toshiba who have loaned appliances and
to all other manufacturers who have helped with the
technical information.*

Foreword

The combination oven has to be the most exciting development on the domestic appliance front in recent years.

The microwave revolutionized our lives. Suddenly we were not tied to the kitchen all day, food could be produced in minutes and reheated without drying out. It could also be quickly defrosted and all this as well as saving on washing up and electricity.

There were, however, limitations, – no browning – no crisping, gone were the days of Sunday roast and Yorkshire puddings, of golden cakes and flaky pastries.

Back we went to the conventional oven for these things. Help arrived not on horseback, but in the guise of a combination oven to rescue us from the disadvantages of a microwave and the slavery of a hot stove. At last you can have the traditional results and the fast cooking time.

In many cases the result is even better than cooking in a conventional oven. You gain the best characteristics of microwave cooking – speed, light texture of cakes, bright vegetable colour, and minimum loss of nutrients together with the best characteristics of conventional cooking – browning, crisping and flavour. The combination of the two cooking methods will particularly benefit family cooking and any recipes which need over 25 minutes cooking time. Dishes such as roast meats, pastries, cakes and breads are greatly improved.

In this book you will find recipes that really do reflect the revolutionary effect a combination oven can have on your cooking.

At a Glance Menu Planner

Fish

Soups, Starters and Light Meals

Meat

Poultry and Game

Vegetables and Vegetarian Meals

Breads and Buns

Cakes
and Biscuits

Hot and Cold
Desserts

Useful Charts

Introduction

WHAT IS A COMBINATION OVEN?

The combination oven gives the choice of at least 3, sometimes as many as 10 cooking methods. Facilities include:

MICROWAVE

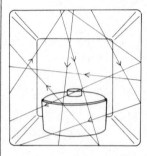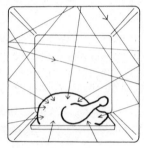

Microwaves are high frequency waves similar to radio and television waves. They are attracted to the moisture in food causing the moisture molecules to vibrate, creating friction, which produces heat to cook food quickly and efficiently. They pass unhindered through materials such as glass, china and certain plastics but are reflected by metal. Microwaves penetrate food to a depth of 3.5 cm (1½ in), producing heat instantaneously. The heat then spreads to the centre of the food by conduction. For this reason standing times are important when the microwave system is used on its own. The microwave system is particularly good for defrosting, reheating, melting, poaching, boiling and simmering.

CONVENTIONAL OVEN

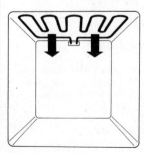

This may either be a fan system or a conventional element system; it is thermostatically controlled and can be used as any other oven. There are certain foods such as batters and biscuits which benefit from cooking solely on this system. In this book where the conventional system is referred to, it should be understood to mean a fan system or conventional element system.

GRILL

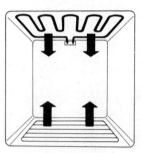

Not all models have this facility. It is a traditional grill element which is useful for toast, steaks and other grilled dishes with very fast cooking time. When combined with the microwave it is especially good for thicker portions of meat, such as chops, sausages and chicken joints. As the grill is not available in all models no recipes in this book call solely for this method.

COMBINATION

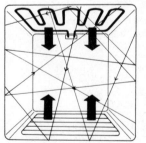

This is where the oven and microwave systems operate *simultaneously*. The conventional heat crisps and browns, while the microwave speeds up the cooking time. This can be used to advantage wherever browning is required.

Some manufacturers permit the use of metal containers. Indeed we got very good results in some ovens using metal, especially for cakes. However, the timings are slightly different. Check with your manufacturer before you use metal and test at the end of the cooking time to see if extra time is required.

Turntables Some ovens have turntables and this will determine the shape of the dish that can be used. In some cases a 2-tier system can be used for baking. Manufacturers may recommend placing an ovenproof plate between the turntable and any metal dishes used.

In combination ovens the microwaves are only part of the cooking process. If in any doubt choose a lower microwave setting and if necessary extend the cooking time slightly. We do, however, find the cooking temperature important to achieve best results and for this reason most of our recipes recommend preheating. Preheating times will vary from manufacturer to manufacturer and may be as little as 5 minutes, or as long as 20 minutes.

ADAPTING YOUR OWN RECIPES

Firstly, try to find a comparable recipe in this book or in your manufacturer's recipe book. If this is not possible, as a general rule of the thumb, use a higher temperature than normal and low power microwave. Check the progress frequently. Make a note of your result for future reference.

FAULT FINDING

FAULT	SUGGESTED REMEDIES
Food not brown enough	1. Check the oven was preheated before cooking. 2. Turn up the temperature next time. 3. Allow a little extra time at the end without the microwave.
Food not cooked but brown enough	1. Raise the microwave power. 2. Cook from a cold start. 3. Lower the oven temperature and cook for slightly longer.
Food brown enough but overcooked	1. Lower microwave power. 2. Shorten microwave time. 3. Add a little extra liquid where appropriate.
Bottom not cooked	1. If a flan, precook base for 5 minutes at 200°C, LOW power microwave before filling. 2. Preheat a metal tray (where manufacturers allow) or glass tray, with the oven and place the container on to this hot tray at the start of cooking.
Cracked cakes	1. Hollow out the top of the cake slightly before cooking.
Excess splashing (meats particularly)	1. Cook in a deeper dish. 2. Drain off any excess fat during cooking. 3. Lower the temperature. 4. Lower the power level.

The recipes in this book are ones that particularly benefit from combination cooking. We hope you enjoy them and that they give you the confidence to experiment further.

TECHNIQUES FOR COMBINATION COOKING

Preheating We have found that the best results are achieved by putting food into a hot oven. Preheating times vary tremendously between different ovens and can be as little as 5 minutes or as much as 20 minutes. Where preheating is specified use only the conventional system. *Do not* preheat using the microwave.

Turning food We have found it beneficial to turn meat and poultry halfway through the cooking period to give even browning. In some ovens it is advisable to turn the dish occasionally to give uniform cooking.

Standing times Whilst these are not as important, as when the microwave is used on its own, foods such as

COOKING UTENSILS

MICROWAVE

Suitable	Unsuitable
glass	lead crystal
glazed ceramic	unglazed earthen ware
china	tupperware
rigid plastic	melamine
boiling bags	metal dishes of any type,
roasting bags	including foil containers and
paper	dishes decorated with gold or
microwave suitable plastic film	silver trim.

CONVENTIONAL COOKING

Suitable	Unsuitable
oven-proof glass eg: pyrex	plastic
oven-proof ceramics	tupperware
metal baking tins and trays	plastic film
cast iron casserole dishes	lead crystal
heat resistant plastic	
earthenware	

COMBINATION COOKING

Be guided by what your manufacturer's instruction book says. Some manufacturers of combination ovens allow the use of certain metal containers but do check with your user's instruction book. The following dishes are suitable for all models.

Suitable	Unsuitable
oven-proof glass	plastic
heat resistant plastic	paper
oven-proof ceramics	metal casseroles with lids

Oven-proof glass, ceramic, or heat resistant plastic containers have been used in all the recipes tested for this book.

HOW TO USE THIS BOOK WITH YOUR OVEN

All our recipes are written for high (600W), medium (300W) and low (180W) power levels. If your oven has different settings the following chart will act as a guide. We have found whilst testing the recipes on various models that quite a wide variation of microwave output achieve similar results.

MAKE OF OVEN	HIGH	MEDIUM	LOW
Bejam BM801	high speed + extra time	high speed	high speed less time
Belling 334	high speed + extra time	high speed	high speed less time
Belling Triplet 333	high	medium	low
Bosch Multimicro HBE 6920 HBE 6900	1	2	3
Bosch HMG 2000 HMG 2200	600	180 + extra time	180
Bosch HMG 2010 HMG 2210	4	3	2
Brother 2000	high	medium	low
Brother 2100	high speed + extra time	high speed	high speed less time
Brother MF2200	high speed + extra time	high speed	high speed less time
Gaggenau	details not available at the time of printing		
Hot Point 6680	600	180 + extra time	180
Miele	600	300	150
Neff 6180 6185	600 600	180 + extra time 180 + extra time	180 180
Panasonic NE972	2 + extra time	2	3
Panasonic NE992/993	2 + extra time	2	3
Scholtes F2860 F2865	5	3 or 2	2 or 1
Sharp 8170 8270	100%	50%	30%
Siemens HF4200 HF4202	600	180 + extra time	180
Siemens HB8704	1	2	3
Siemens HF6504 HF6502	4 4	3 3	1 1
Toshiba ER9610	high	med–med low	med low–low

meats will carve more easily if left to rest after cooking for 10 minutes to firm up; before turning out cakes should be left for 5 minutes in the dish which they were cooked in. Where the microwave is used on its own follow recommended standing times.

Covering Most food cooked in the combination oven should be left uncovered to achieve the best browning. Where covering is recommended in recipes, such as casseroles, use heatproof non-metalic lids. Do not use plastic film or aluminium foil.

Stirring May be recommended in some recipes, where the microwave is used on its own, or in casseroles and stews. In other types of combination cooking it is not generally necessary.

Soups, Starters and Light Meals

The use of the combination oven means that an endless variety
of soups, starters and light meals can be prepared with ease and in the minimum of time.
Although cooking times of soups are not much reduced in the microwave, the
amount of effort put in by the cook in constantly watching and stirring is
minimized. Colours of vegetables will remain brighter, and if a crispy topping to
make the soup more substantial is desired, the combination system can be used
to good effect.

A hot starter to a meal can be delicious, especially during winter months, but they
are often avoided at dinner parties because of a last minute rush in the kitchen.
With the help of the combination oven, freshly cooked gratin type dishes can be
prepared and served in the time it would take you to slice a melon! Here is a
selection of tasty lunch or supper dishes which are both appetising and
quick to prepare.

COUNTRY MUSHROOM SOUP WITH A PUFF PASTRY LID

Soups are usually best made in the microwave, however this one has a puff pastry lid and so is very suited to the talents of a combination oven. It is very filling and makes a better supper dish than a starter. You need some oven proof soup bowls to cook it in.

Serves 4

25 g (1 oz) butter

1 medium onion, finely chopped

grated rind of a lemon

50 g (2 oz) fresh wholemeal breadcrumbs

15 ml (1 level tbsp) fresh parsley, chopped

pinch mixed herbs

1 vegetable stock cube

salt and pepper

small packet puff pastry

egg or milk for brushing

1. Put the butter and onions in a large bowl and microwave on HIGH for 3 minutes.

2. Add the chopped mushrooms, stir and microwave on HIGH for 3 minutes.

3. Stir in the lemon rind, breadcrumbs, parsley and herbs. Divide the mixture between 4 oven proof soup bowls.

4. Make the stock cube up to 750 ml (1¼ pt) with boiling water; pour into the bowls. Check the seasoning.

5. Roll the pastry out to make lids; use the trimmings to put a strip round the rims to stick the lid onto. Brush the lids with milk or egg. Bake in a preheated oven 200°C, MEDIUM power microwave for 12 minutes or until golden brown.

——— COOK'S TIP ———
Preheat the oven while you are microwaving the mushrooms. Make sure you do not stretch the pastry otherwise it will fall into the bowls – still delicious but it does not look quite so good. Remember the soup will be boiling when it comes out of the oven and the lid keeps the heat in, so do not rush too fast to eat it.

See photograph page 25

FRENCH ONION SOUP

Whilst this is not strictly a combination oven recipe, it is one where the features of an oven and microwave can be used. Cooking the soup in a microwave instead of in a saucepan does mean it needs very little attention. If you have time, make this in advance the day before, the flavours will really develop and reheating will be easy in the combination oven.

Serves 4

450 g (1 lb) onions, thinly sliced

30 ml (2 tbsp) olive oil

50 g (2 oz) butter

12 g (½ oz) flour

900 ml (1½ pt) beef stock (use 2 quality cubes)

bay leaf

pepper and salt

4 slices of French bread

4 slices of Gruyere

1. Put the onions in a large bowl with the butter and oil. Microwave on HIGH power for 15 minutes, stirring once.

2. Add the flour and cook for a further 2 minutes on HIGH.

3. Stir in the stock which should be hot, add the bay leaf then microwave on HIGH for 10 minutes, stirring once.

4. Put the bread into a hot oven at 200°C, or under the grill and brown lightly on both sides.

5. Ladle the cold soup into 4 bowls. Place a slice of bread and a slice of cheese on top of each bowl. Put into the preheated oven at 220°C, MEDIUM power microwave for 10 minutes or until the soup is hot and the cheese is bubbling.

RABBIT AND PISTACHIO TERRINE

This dish will serve 8 generously as a starter or 6 as a main course with salad in the summer. It will freeze if you have any left over but is better unfrozen. Make it at least a day before you need it, for the flavours to develop and serve it sliced so the lovely colours can be admired. The combination oven does away with the need for a water bath and it is cooked very quickly.

Serves 8 as starter
Serves 6 as main course

1 small rabbit boned or 450 g (1 lb) boned rabbit meat
30 ml (2 tbsp) brandy
25 g (1 oz) butter
1 large clove garlic
1 small onion, finely chopped
45 g (1 lb) minced belly pork
1 fresh bay leaf, chopped
2.5 ml (½ tsp) thyme
salt and pepper
1 egg
50 g (2 oz) pistachios (optional)
200 g (½ lb) streaky bacon

1. Put the rabbit breast fillets in the brandy and leave to soak for a couple of hours.

2. Melt the butter in a bowl and microwave the garlic and onion on HIGH for 3 minutes.

3. Mince the rabbit, excluding the breast fillets, the pork, the chopped bayleaf, onion and garlic.

4. Add the brandy, seasonings, egg and thyme to the mixture. Make a small meat ball, microwave on HIGH for 1 minute. Taste to check seasoning.

5. Put the pistachio nuts in boiling water for 1 minute and then skin.

6. Take the rind off the bacon and stretch the rashers with the back of a knife.

7. Use the bacon to line a 900 ml (1½ pt) glass or combination oven proof oblong dish.

8. Pack in half the minced mixture. Place the fillets in a line down the centre and arrange the pistachios on either side. Pack in the rest of the minced mixture. Cover with grease-proof paper and cook at 170°C, LOW power microwave for 35 minutes.

9. Cool slightly then place a board on top. Put 1 kg (2 lb) in weight on the board and leave overnight.

10. Turn out and serve.

See cover photograph

PATE EN CROUTE WITH CUMBERLAND SAUCE

A very impressive starter which looks as if it is difficult to make but isn't. It is one of our favourite dishes to demonstrate, proving very popular with our course members at the Cookery School! Without a combination oven this recipe would be time consuming. No such problem when the microwave is helping the cooking along. Do not miss out the sauce, it is so good and goes very well with other meats such as gammon.

Serves 6

Pastry

20 g (¾ oz) lard
225 ml (¼ pt) milk
225 g (6 oz) plain flour

Filling

100 g (4 oz) lambs liver, finely chopped
220 g (8 oz) sausage meat
220 g (8 oz) lean pork, minced
1 small onion, finely chopped
1 clove garlic, crushed
2.5 ml (½ tsp) sage
15 ml (1 tbsp) sherry
salt and black pepper

To glaze

1 egg beaten

Cumberland sauce

Cumberland sauce

150 ml (¼ pt) red wine

30 ml (2 tbsp) redcurrant jelly

rind and juice of ½ orange

rind and juice of ½ lemon

5 ml (1 level tsp) arrowroot

1. Line a 450 g (1 lb) loaf tin with cling-film.

2. Mix together all the filling ingredients in a bowl and leave to stand while preparing the pastry.

3. Place the lard and milk in a bowl and microwave on HIGH for 3 minutes.

4. Place the flour in a mixing bowl and pour over the boiling milk and lard. Mix with a wooden spoon and then knead lightly to form a smooth dough.

5. Cut off ⅓ of the pastry and reserve for the lid then place the remaining pastry in the loaf tin and mould up the sides.

6. Pack the filling into the pastry shell and brush around the edge with the beaten egg.

7. Roll out the remaining pastry and place over the filling, sealing the edges firmly. Use any trimmings to make pastry leaves for the top.

8. Carefully lift out the pate using the cling-film and place on the baking sheet. Slide out of the cling-film.

9. Make a small hole in the centre of the pie to allow steam to escape. Brush all over with the beaten egg and decorate with the pastry leaves.

10. Cook in a preheated oven at 220°C, LOW power microwave for 20 minutes then remove and allow to cool. Chill.

CUMBERLAND SAUCE

1. Place the wine, redcurrant jelly, rind and juice of the orange and lemon in a jug and heat in the microwave on HIGH for 3 minutes. Stir until the jelly is dissolved.

2. Blend the arrowroot with a little water and stir into the juice. Return to the oven and heat on HIGH for a further minute.

3. Leave the sauce to cool then serve chilled with the pate.

See photograph page 27

SCALLOP AND PRAWN SHELLS

For shell fish lovers, a starter which cannot be resisted! Although fresh scallops are not always easy to come by, we find most freezer centres sell bags of frozen ones. These should be thoroughly defrosted, as should the prawns if frozen ones are used, and well drained on kitchen paper. Wet shell fish will make a very thin sauce, which may bubble over.

Serves 6

150 g (6 oz) king or queen scallops

150 g (6 oz) prawns

150 ml (¼ pt) double cream

25 ml (1½ tbsp) white wine

10 ml (1 level tsp) parsley, chopped

salt and freshly ground black pepper

675 g (1½ lb) potatoes, peeled, boiled and mashed with butter and milk

To garnish

Lemon slices and parsley sprigs

1. If king scallops are used, slice, and divide with the prawns between 6 scallop shell dishes or other shallow dishes.

2. Whip the cream and white wine until just beginning to thicken, then stir in the parsley and seasoning. Spoon over scallops and prawns.

3. Pipe the potatoes around the shells then bake in a preheated oven at 220°C, LOW power microwave for 10 minutes. Serve garnished with lemon slices and parsley.

―――― **VARIATION** ――――
White fish such as plaice or sole could be used instead of scallops. The dish is successfully cooked using the grill and microwave if this combination is available.

See photograph page 27

CRAB AND SWEETCORN RAMEKINS

No starter could be simpler, yet more delicious than this! We used parmesan cheese for the topping which goes well with the flavour of crab, but for those who do not like the smell, any grated cheese will do. It can be prepared in advance, then popped into the oven as the guests are about to sit down. Serve with warm wholemeal bread or toast.

Serves 6

1 × 170 g (6 oz) tin crabmeat
1 × 198 g (7 oz) tin sweetcorn with peppers
150 ml (¼ pt) double cream
salt and pepper
25 g (1 oz) breadcrumbs
15 g (½ oz) grated parmesan or other cheese

1. Drain the crabmeat and sweetcorn, then divide between 6 ramekin dishes.

2. Season cream with salt and black pepper, then pour over the crab and sweetcorn.

3. Mix together the breadcrumbs and cheese and sprinkle over the ramekins. Bake in a preheated oven at 225°C, LOW power microwave for 10 minutes. Serve immediately.

—— VARIATION ——
Prawns and tiny sliced button mushrooms can be used in place of the crab and sweetcorn.

PLAICE FILO ROLLS

Filo pastry is becoming more readily available from delicatessens around the country, and is well worth experimenting with as it is so easy to handle. Despite its delicate appearance, the pastry is fairly tough and has the advantage of really sealing in the filling. This extremely tasty recipe was thought up in a panicky moment when we wanted to make 3 plaice fillets feed 6 hungry people as a starter! It worked very well!

Serves 6

15 g (½ oz) butter
30 ml (2 tbsp) onion, finely chopped
50 g (2 oz) button mushrooms, finely chopped
25 g (1 oz) fresh white breadcrumbs
10 ml (2 tsp) parsley, chopped
1 small egg, lightly beaten
15–30 ml (1–2 tbsp) single cream or top of the milk
salt and freshly ground black pepper
3 large plaice fillets
melted butter
6 sheets filo pastry

1. Melt the butter in a bowl in the microwave on HIGH power for 30 seconds. Stir in the onion and mushroom and return to the microwave on HIGH power for 2 minutes.

2. Stir in the breadcrumbs, parsley, egg, cream and seasoning.

3. Skin the plaice fillets and cut in half lengthways. Place a spoonful of mushroom mixture onto each piece of fish and fold in half.

4. Put a stuffed plaice fillet on a corner of 2 sheets of filo pastry and roll up, folding over the sides to form a neat parcel. Repeat with the remaining fish.

5. Arrange the parcels on a baking dish, brush generously with melted butter and cook in a preheated oven at 220°C, LOW power microwave for 10–15 minutes, brushing with more butter halfway through the cooking time.

See photograph page 45

MUSHROOM SOUFFLE FLAN

This is a delicious flan based on a French recipe. We use it as a starter or during the summer as a main course. One of us served this in the garden one lovely summer day, dishing out 4 generous starter-size portions which were eaten very quickly. The guests looked at the remaining flan and said it was so good it would be a shame not to finish it, so they did – then they carried on to the main course. The proof of the pudding is in the eating and this one has been very popular.

Serves 8 as starter
Serves 4 as main course

225 g (8 oz) plain flour

125 g (4 oz) butter

1 egg yolk

60 ml (4 tbsp) water

100 ml (4 fl oz) white wine

50 g (2 oz) butter

2 shallots, finely chopped

275 g (10 oz) button mushrooms, sliced

15 g (½ oz) flour

125 g (4 oz) smoked ham

2 tomatoes, skinned and deseeded

15 ml (1 level tbsp) fresh chives, chopped

15 ml (1 level tbsp) tarragon, fresh if possible

150 ml (6 fl oz) double cream

2 eggs, separated

salt and pepper

1. Rub the butter into the flour until it resembles fine breadcrumbs.

2. Mix the egg yolk and water together, add to the flour and mix to a dough adding a little extra water if necessary.

3. Roll out the pastry and use to line a 25 cm (10 in) flan dish.

4. Put the wine in a cup and microwave on HIGH for about 5 minutes, until reduced by half.

5. Melt the butter in a large bowl on HIGH for 1 minute, add shallots and saute on HIGH for 2 minutes.

6. Add the sliced mushrooms and microwave on HIGH for 2 minutes stirring once. Add flour.

7. Mix in the ham, the chopped tomato flesh, herbs, cream, egg yolks and seasoning.

8. Bake the flan case in a preheated oven at 190°C, LOW power microwave for 5 minutes.

9. Whisk egg whites until stiff and fold into the filling; pour into the flan case.

10. Bake at 190°C, LOW power microwave for 20 minutes.

CRISPY TOPPED MUSHROOMS

These delicious, creamy mushrooms are a firm favourite as a starter at dinner parties. They can be cooked in individual dishes, in which case, cut the cooking time down to 3–4 minutes. Try to choose small button mushrooms, but if these are not available, quarter or halve larger ones.

Serves 4

450 g (1 lb) button mushrooms

100 g (4 oz) smoked back bacon, derinded and chopped

150 ml (¼ pt) double cream

45 ml (3 tbsp) medium sherry

salt and black pepper

100 g (4 oz) wholemeal breadcrumbs

25 g (1 oz) butter

1. Wipe and trim the mushrooms, then place in a buttered dish.

2. Stir in the bacon, cream and sherry, and season to taste.

3. Sprinkle with breadcrumbs, dot with butter and cook in a preheated oven at 200°C, MEDIUM power microwave for 15 minutes. Serve piping hot.

HAM AND ASPARAGUS QUICHE

If you are over enthusiastic with the quantities of asparagus you cook and find yourself with leftovers, the following recipe will help you use them up. You can then freeze the quiches and bring them out during the winter months to the delight of family and friends.

Serves 4–6

Pastry

150 g (6 oz) plain flour
pinch of salt
75 g (3 oz) margarine or margarine and lard
30 ml (2 tbsp) water

Filling

125 g (4 oz) ham
1 small tin asparagus spears, drained
2 eggs
milk or cream
salt and pepper

1. To make the pastry, sieve the flour and salt into the mixing bowl. Rub the fat into the flour until the mixture resembles fine breadcrumbs, then stir in the water with a knife.

2. Knead lightly with the fingers until a smooth dough is formed, then turn on to a floured surface.

3. Roll out the pastry and use to line a 20 cm (8 in) flan dish. Prick the base with a fork.

4. Roughly chop the ham and spread over the pastry base. Arrange the asparagus spears over the top.

5. Beat the eggs in a measuring jug and make up to 300 ml (½ pt) with milk or cream. Season with salt and black pepper, then pour over the ham and asparagus.

6. Bake in a preheated oven at 200°C for 25 minutes. Serve warm.

See photograph page 26

HAM AND TOMATO GOUGERE

We love making choux pastry and use it in recipes wherever possible! Although it is very successful cooked by combination as a gougere, do not be tempted to try cooking choux buns or eclairs in the same way. Stick to the conventional or fan system for these. The following recipe is ideal as a supper dish or a starter to a meal. For a starter, it can be cooked in individual dishes, in which case the cooking time will be a little shorter.

Serves 4

25 g (1 oz) butter
1 small onion, finely chopped
100 g (4 oz) chicken livers, chopped
100 g (4 oz) button mushrooms, sliced
100 g (4 oz) ham, roughly chopped
4 tomatoes, skinned and chopped
15 ml (1 level tbsp) plain flour
300 ml (1½ pt) hot chicken stock
15 ml (1 tbsp) tomato puree
salt and black pepper

Choux pastry

150 ml (¼ pt) water
50 g (2 oz) butter
65 g (2½ oz) plain flour
2 eggs, lightly beaten
50 g (2 oz) grated cheese

1. Melt the butter in a shallow oval or oblong dish approximately 25 cm (10 in) long, on HIGH power for 1 minute.

2. Stir in the onion, liver and mushrooms and cook on HIGH power for 3 minutes, stirring halfway through the cooking time.

3. Add the ham and tomatoes then stir in the flour and gradually blend in the stock and tomato puree. Cook on HIGH power for 3 minutes, then stir thoroughly and season to taste.

4. To make the choux pastry, place the water and butter in a bowl and heat in the microwave on HIGH

power for 4 minutes or until boiling and the butter is melted.

5. Shoot in flour and beat until the mixture leaves the side of the bowl. Cool slightly, then beat in the eggs a little at a time.

6. Stir in the cheese then pipe or spoon around the edge of the dish containing the ham and tomato mixture. Cook in a preheated oven at 200°C, LOW power microwave for 18 minutes.

QUICHE LORRAINE

Despite the book 'Real men don't eat Quiche', this traditional recipe never fails to please! Quiches freeze extremely well, but should always be served warm after defrosting.

Serves 6

Pastry

150 g (6 oz) plain flour

pinch of salt

75 g (3 oz) margarine or lard and margarine

30 ml (2 tbsp) water

Filling

15 g (½ oz) butter

1 small onion, finely chopped

100 g (4 oz) bacon, chopped

100 g (4 oz) grated cheese

2 eggs

single cream or milk

salt and black pepper

1. Sieve the flour and salt into a bowl and rub in the fat until the mixture resembles fine breadcrumbs. Stir in the water then knead lightly to a smooth dough.

2. Roll out the pastry on a floured surface and use to line a 20 cm (8 in) flan dish. Prick the base with a fork.

3. Melt butter in a bowl on HIGH power for ½ minute, then stir in the onion and bacon and cook on HIGH power for 3 minutes. Drain off any fat, then

spoon into the base of the flan, and sprinkle over the cheese.

4. Lightly whisk the eggs in a measuring jug, then make up to 300 ml (½ pt) with cream or milk. Season to taste, then pour over the cheese. Bake in a preheated oven at 200°C, LOW power microwave for 20 minutes or until golden brown. Serve hot or cold.

CHEESE AND SAGE PUDDING

This is a cross between a souffle and a savoury bread pudding. It is light and fluffy and makes an ideal supper dish for the family. If you grow your own herbs, use fresh sage instead of dried, increasing the quantity to 10 ml (2 tsp).

Serves 4

125 g (4 oz) fresh wholemeal breadcrumbs

600 ml (1 pt) milk

2 eggs, separated

125 g (4 oz) grated cheese

15 ml (1 level tbsp) onion, finely chopped

2.5 ml (½ tsp) sage

2.5 ml (½ tsp) dried mustard

salt and black pepper

1. Place breadcrumbs in a buttered 1.8 lit (2 pt) souffle dish.

2. Heat the milk in the microwave on HIGH power for 4 minutes. Pour over the breadcrumbs and leave to soak for 30 minutes.

3. Beat the egg yolks lightly and stir into the mixture with the cheese, onion, sage, mustard and seasoning. Mix thoroughly.

4. Whisk the egg whites until stiff, then fold into the cheese mixture. Bake in a preheated oven at 200°C, MEDIUM power microwave for 15 minutes. Serve with fresh vegetables or salad.

CHEESE SOUFFLE

This souffle may be fractionally inferior to one baked traditionally, but its speed and its ability to keep two small boys standing in silent fascination for seven whole minutes watching it rise, make it well worth including in the book! If you want to cook it traditionally, it will take approximately 25 minutes in an oven preheated to 200°C.

Serves 4

25 g (1 oz) butter

25 g (1 oz) flour

200 ml (7 fl oz) milk

100 g (4 oz) grated cheese

2.5 ml (½ tsp) mustard powder

pinch of cayenne pepper

salt and black pepper

4 eggs, separated

1. Place the butter in a bowl and microwave on HIGH for 1 minute. Stir in the flour then blend in the milk. Cook on HIGH power for 3 minutes, whisking halfway through the cooking time, and again at the end.

2. Beat in the grated cheese, mustard, seasoning and egg yolks.

3. Whisk the egg whites until stiff, then fold into the cheese sauce. Pour into a buttered 1.2 lit (2 pt) souffle dish and bake in a preheated oven at 250°C, HIGH power microwave for 7 minutes. Serve immediately.

—— ALTERNATIVE ——
Add 125 g (4 oz) of either chopped mushrooms or cooked smoked fish, in place of the cheese, if preferred.

QUICK PIZZA

Using a scone base for the pizza considerably speeds up the making, and using a combination oven speeds up the cooking. A double saving! Try decorating quarters, with the eater's favourite toppings – no more arguments!

Serves 4

Base

225 g (8 oz) self raising flour

5 ml (1 level tsp) baking powder

50 g (2 oz) margarine

150 ml (¼ pt) skimmed milk

Topping

45 ml (3 tbsp) tomato puree

½ onion, grated

5 ml (1 level tsp) mixed herbs

salt and pepper

50 g (2 oz) sweetcorn

50 g (2 oz) mushrooms, sliced

200 g (8 oz) cheese, grated

4 rashers of bacon, derinded

10 olives (optional)

1. Sieve the flour and baking powder together.

2. Rub the fat into the flour until it resembles breadcrumbs then add milk and mix the dough, until firm.

3. Grease a baking sheet suitable for your oven, and roll the pastry out to 2.5 cm (½ in) thick in either a circle or a rectangle. Place on the baking sheet.

4. Mix together the puree, onion, herbs, salt and pepper and spread thinly over the base.

5. Sprinkle with the vegetables and cover with cheese, then decorate with strips of bacon and dot with olives.

6. Cook at 210°C, LOW power microwave for 15–20 minutes.

See photograph page 26

Fish

In recent years, fish has been very underused, mainly due to the disappearance of many wet fish shops from the high street. Now more fish shops are appearing again and a lot of the larger supermarkets have a fresh fish counter where the selection of fish is growing. Take advantage of this and try something new.

Fish can play an important part in healthy eating. It is easily digested and highly nutritious, and therefore deserves a prominent place on the weekly menu. Indeed, as people have become more conscious of their diet and restricting intake of fat, both white and oily fish have become more popular.

The microwave system is ideal for poaching fish, maintaining the delicate flavour and texture, but it can be limiting. Many fish dishes benefit from a crisp skin or topping, so by using the combination oven, you can expand your range of recipes.

SALMON JALOUSIE

This makes a colourful lunch, and is very economical to make using tinned salmon. If you feel extravagant, do use fresh salmon. The combination oven helps the pastry puff up beautifully without toughening the filling.

Serves 4

| 150 ml (¼ pt) milk |
| ½ onion |
| bay leaf |
| 25 g (1 oz) butter |
| 25 g (1 oz) flour |
| salt and pepper |
| 175 g (6 oz) frozen petit pois |
| 213 g (7½ oz) tin salmon |
| 2 tomatoes, sliced |
| 350 g (12 oz) puff pastry |
| egg for brushing |

1. Put the milk, bay leaf and onion in a jug and microwave for 3 minutes on HIGH. Leave to stand for 20 minutes.

2. Remove the onion and bay leaf and discard. Add the butter and flour and mix well. Microwave on HIGH power for 2 minutes, beat well until smooth and microwave on HIGH for another 2 minutes.

3. Beat the sauce well again, add the frozen peas and the juice from the tin of salmon, stir and season.

4. Divide the pastry into two unequal halves, roll the smaller half out to a rectangle 22.5×20 cm (9×8 in). Roll the larger half to a rectangle 25×22.5 cm (10×9 in).

5. Fold the larger rectangle in half longways and cut from the centre to the edge at 1 cm (½ in) intervals being careful to leave 2.5 cm (1 in) uncut round the edge. Unfold.

6. Place the uncut piece of pastry on a baking dish or tray. Spread the sauce mixture leaving 2.5 cm (1 in) round the edge. Pile on the flaked fish then the sliced tomatoes.

7. Put the other cut piece of pastry on top; damp the edges to seal.

8. Brush with the egg and bake in a preheated oven at 200°C, 5 minutes HIGH power microwave and 12 minutes LOW power or until golden brown, or 20 minutes LOW power.

--- **VARIATION** ---

Use tuna and sweetcorn instead of the salmon and peas, if preferred.

TROUT WITH GREEN SAUCE

Some years ago, we stayed with friends on their trout farm in Wiltshire. They were just setting up the farm, so we worked hard all weekend, planting hedges, feeding fish etc. Our reward at the end of the weekend was a car full of trout. We had trout served in every possible way, and this turned out to be the favourite.

Serves 4

| 4 trout |
| lemon juice |
| salt and freshly ground black pepper |
| 15 ml (1 level tbsp) fresh chives, chopped |
| 10 ml (2 level tsp) parsley, chopped |
| 15 ml (1 tbsp) white wine |
| 150 ml (¼ pt) double cream |
| salt and freshly ground black pepper |
| 15 ml (1 tbsp) fresh white breadcrumbs |

1. Gut the trout, then wash thoroughly and dry on kitchen paper. Sprinkle inside with lemon juice and a little seasoning.

2. Place the fish in a shallow dish, then sprinkle over the chives, parsley and white wine.

3. Add a little seasoning to the cream then pour over the fish. Sprinkle over the breadcrumbs and bake in a preheated oven at 230°C, LOW power microwave for 10 minutes.

COD AND MUSHROOMS EN CROUTE

This is easy but impressive. It makes a substantial fish dish either for a dinner party or everyday. We use cod fillets for this; if they are frozen defrost them and drain well. Using the combination oven the taste is wonderful, the fish is full of flavour and perfectly cooked without being dry. The recipe serves 4 very well; if you want to feed 6 just use another cod fillet and roll the pastry a little bigger.

Serves 4–6

25 g (1 oz) butter

1 large clove of garlic

1 small onion, finely chopped

175 g (6 oz) button mushrooms, chopped

¼ whole nutmeg, grated

1.25 ml (¼ tsp) dried tarragon

salt and freshly ground black pepper

450 g (1 lb) puff pastry

675 g (1½ lb) cod fillets, skinned

1 egg

1. Place the butter, crushed garlic and onion in a bowl and microwave on HIGH for 3 minutes stirring once.

2. Add the mushrooms and microwave on HIGH for 3 minutes.

3. Add the nutmeg and tarragon and season well.

4. Roll the pastry out to a large oblong about 30 cm × 40 cm (12 in × 16 in), trim the edges and keep the trimmings.

5. Put half the mushroom mixture down the centre of the pastry, lay on the cod fillets seasoning as you go and, trying to keep even thickness, top with remaining mushrooms.

6. Fold the pastry over and damp to seal well. Decorate with leaves made from trimmings.

7. Brush twice with the beaten egg and bake in a preheated oven 190°C, LOW power microwave for 16–20 minutes, until golden brown.

BAKED CODLING

Nothing is simpler and looks more splendid than a whole cooked fish. We chose codling because it is reasonably priced and readily available. Having said that, it is a good idea to order it from your fishmonger in advance. Cooked in a combination oven, the skin crisps and the flesh remains incredibly moist. It has a colourful Mediterranean style sauce to go with it. When available, sea bass or grey mullet can be used in place of the codling.

Serves 6

1 × 900 g–1.1 kg (2–2½ lb) codling, gutted

salt and black pepper

lemon juice

50 g (2 oz) butter

50 g (2 oz) smoked bacon, cut into thin strips

1 large red pepper, deseeded and sliced

350 g (12 oz) tomatoes, skinned and chopped

150 ml (¼ pt) double cream

5 ml (1 tsp) mustard

1. Wash the fish thoroughly inside and out, then dry with kitchen paper. Season inside and out with salt, pepper and lemon juice.

2. Butter a large, shallow dish, then place the fish in it. Lay the bacon strips on the fish.

3. Arrange the vegetables around the fish, dot with the remaining butter and bake in a preheated oven at 225°C, LOW power microwave for 13 minutes.

4. Stir the mustard into the cream, then pour over the vegetables, and cook for a further 2 minutes at 225°C, LOW power microwave. Serve the fish whole on a platter with the vegetables and sauce arranged around it.

———— COOK'S TIP ————
For ovens with turntables, the head may need to be removed from the fish.

See photograph page 28

BUTTERED COD AND POTATO LAYER

This is a very economical easy supper dish to make. All it needs to go with it are some green vegetables or salad.

Serves 4

Sauce

300 ml (½ pt) milk
bay leaf
slice of onion
75 g (3 oz) butter
25 g (1 oz) flour
15 ml (1 level tbsp) parsley, chopped
salt and pepper

Base

675 g (1½ lb) potatoes, peeled, coarsley grated and rinsed
450 g (1 lb) cod
25 g (1 oz) grated cheddar
little extra butter to grease the dish

1. Heat the milk, bay leaf and onion in the microwave on HIGH for 3½ minutes. Leave to stand for 20 minutes before removing the bay leaf and onion.

2. Add 25 g (1 oz) of the butter and flour to the milk. Mix well and microwave on HIGH for 3 minutes, beating well halfway and again at the end. The sauce should be smooth and thick.

3. Gradually add the other 50 g (2 oz) of the butter, the seasoning and parsley.

4. Grease a 20 cm (8 in) dish, put in a ⅓ of the potato and season.

5. Cut the fish into 4 cm (1½ in) cubes. Place on the potato. Pour over the sauce, top with the rest of the potato, season and sprinkle with cheese.

6. Bake in a preheated oven at 200°C, LOW power for 35–40 minutes or until tender when a knife is inserted in the centre.

HALIBUT AND CIDER PIE

Halibut is a delicate fish with a good flavour which blends well with the other ingredients in this recipe. Do not be put off, however if this fish is not available as any other white fish can be used instead, such as cod, hake or haddock. For teetotalers or those with children, apple juice can replace the cider.

Serves 4

450 g (1 lb) halibut steaks
salt and pepper
125 g (4 oz) button mushrooms, sliced
225 g (8 oz) tomatoes, skinned and sliced
25 g (1 oz) butter
25 g (1 oz) flour
300 ml (½ pt) cider
75 g (3 oz) grated cheese
675 g (1½ lb) potatoes, peeled, boiled and mashed with butter and milk

1. Wash and dry the halibut and remove the skin and as many bones as possible. Place in the bottom of a 1.8 lit (3 pt) casserole or souffle dish.

2. Season the fish then cover with the sliced mushrooms and tomatoes.

3. Melt the butter on HIGH for 1 minute, then stir in the flour and gradually blend in the cider. Return to the microwave and cook for 4 minutes on HIGH, stirring halfway through the cooking time and again on completion.

4. Season the sauce, then pour over the tomatoes. Pipe or fork the potato over the top and cook in a preheated oven at 200°C, LOW power microwave for 20 minutes.

Left to right: Cheese topped bacon and onion bread (page 91); Country mushroom soup with puff pastry lid (page 13); Tuna and pasta bake (page 31); Stuffed cabbage leaves (page 72).

OVERLEAF
Left to right: Ham and asparagus quiche (page 18); Quick pizza (page 20); Scallop and prawn shells (page 15); Pate en croute with cumberland sauce (page 14).

HADDOCK AND CHEESE SOUFFLE

In a combination oven a souffle rises quickly and evenly but high power must be used otherwise the pulsing of the power causes the souffle to rise and fall and rise and fall and stay there! Get the oven as hot as you can and ask your guests to sit down at table and wait.

Serves 4

25 g (1 oz) butter

25 g (1 oz) flour

240 ml (8 fl oz) milk

75 g (3 oz) cheddar cheese, grated

3 eggs, separated

225 g (8 oz) smoked haddock, skinned

salt and pepper

1. Put the milk, butter and flour in a jug and microwave on HIGH power for 2 minutes, then beat well. Microwave on HIGH for a further 2 minutes, beat until smooth and thick.

2. Add the cheese, egg yolks and 50 g (2 oz) of the fish, cut very small, season with a little salt and more black pepper to taste.

3. Put the remaining fish, cut into cubes, in the bottom of a 20 cm (8 in) souffle dish that has been well buttered.

4. Whisk the egg whites, until thick and fold in the cheese mixture. Pile on top of the fish in the souffle dish.

5. Bake the souffle in a very hot oven, preheated to 240°C, HIGH power microwave for 8–10 minutes, when it will be golden and set.

--- **SERVING SUGGESTION** ---
A lovely salad makes a good accompaniment for a starter or add crusty bread or baked potatoes in their jackets for a substantial supper.

Baked codling (page 23) with Pommes Anna (page 69).

SMOKED HADDOCK QUICHE

This is always a firm favourite both with friends and at demonstrations. If we could have £1 for every time we have been asked for this recipe (or so the saying goes!) we should be very wealthy indeed. It is delicious as a starter to a meal or as a light supper dish and should always be served warm. It can be frozen and reheated very successfully.

Serves 6

Pastry

150 g (6 oz) plain flour

pinch of salt

75 g (3 oz) lard or margarine

30 ml (2 tbsp) water

Filling

225 g (8 oz) smoked haddock

milk

125 g (4 oz) grated cheese

2 eggs

black pepper

1. To make the pastry, sieve the flour and salt into a mixing bowl. Rub the fat into the flour until the mixture resembles fine breadcrumbs, then stir in the water with a knife.

2. Knead lightly with the fingers until a smooth dough is formed then turn onto a floured surface.

3. Roll out the pastry, and use to line a 20 cm (8 in) flan dish. Prick the base with a fork.

4. Skin the fish, then place in a dish with 15 ml (1 tbsp) milk, cover and microwave on HIGH power for 3–4 minutes. Drain, reserving any liquid.

5. Flake the fish then spread over the base of the pastry. Cover with grated cheese.

6. Beat the eggs in a measuring jug and make up to 300 ml (½ pt) with the liquid from the fish and additional milk. Season with black pepper then pour over the fish and cheese.

7. Bake in a preheated oven at 200°C, LOW power microwave for 20–25 minutes or until set and golden brown.

HADDOCK AND PRAWN COBBLER

We once had seafood pancakes with beansprouts in a restaurant and thought how well the flavours and textures mixed, hence the combination in this recipe. This and the scone topping makes an unusual and delicious fish pie. Sweetcorn, peas or mushrooms can be used in place of the beansprouts, if desired.

Serves 4

40 g (1½ oz) butter
40 g (1½ oz) flour
45 ml (3 tbsp) white wine
15 ml (1 tbsp) lemon juice
approximately 300 ml (½ pt) milk
225 g (8 oz) fresh haddock, skinned and cubed
125 g (4 oz) peeled prawns
1 small tin beansprouts, drained
15 ml (1 level tbsp) parsley, chopped
salt and pepper

Topping

225 g (8 oz) self raising flour
pinch of salt
50 g (2 oz) butter
50 g (2 oz) grated cheese
150 ml (¼ pt) milk

To glaze

extra milk or beaten egg

1. Place the butter in a 1.8 lit (3 pt) souffle dish and melt on HIGH for 1½ minutes.

2. Stir in the flour. Make the wine and lemon juice up to 450 ml (¾ pt) with milk and blend into the roux. Return to the oven and cook on HIGH power for 5 minutes whisking thoroughly halfway through the cooking time, and again on completion. Stir in the remaining ingredients.

3. To make the topping, place the flour and salt in a mixing bowl and rub in the butter, until the mixture resembles fine breadcrumbs.

4. Stir in the grated cheese and milk. Knead lightly to form a smooth dough.

5. Roll out the dough on a floured surface to a thickness of approximately 1.25 cm (½ in), then cut into rounds with a 5 cm (2 in) cutter.

6. Arrange the scones on top of the fish mixture, overlapping each other and covering the whole mixture. Brush with milk or beaten egg and cook at 220°C, LOW power microwave for 20 minutes.

See photograph page 45

LEMON HERRING WITH MUSTARD SAUCE

Herring are delicately flavoured but very bony. For this reason, the backbone should be removed if possible. The sharpness of the lemon stuffing and mustard sauce go particularly well with this economical and rather underused fish.

Serves 4

4 herring
salt and pepper
50 g (2 oz) fresh breadcrumbs
grated rind and juice of ½ lemon
15 ml (1 level tbsp) parsley, chopped
25 g (1 oz) butter, melted

Sauce

75 g (3 oz) butter
10 ml (2 tsp) Dijon mustard
15 ml (1 level tbsp) parsley, chopped
5 ml (1 tsp) lemon juice

1. Gut the herrings and cut off heads if desired. Wash thoroughly, then dry with kitchen paper.

2. Open the herring up on a chopping board with the back uppermost, then press firmly with the thumb all the way down the backbone. Turn over the fish and remove the backbone by slipping a knife under it. Repeat with all the fish.

3. Mix together the breadcrumbs, rind and juice of

the lemon, parsley and half the butter. Use to stuff the fish, then reshape and secure with cocktail sticks.

4. Place in a buttered shallow dish, then brush with remaining butter and cook in a preheated oven at 220°C, LOW power microwave for 10 minutes, or until the fish flakes.

5. To make the sauce, melt the butter on HIGH in the microwave for 1½–2 minutes. Beat in the remaining ingredients and serve with the fish.

TUNA AND PASTA BAKE

This is a colourful dish with an unusual yoghurt topping. The multi-coloured pasta bows never fail to please children who spend ages over the meal, arranging them in different patterns! Do use other pasta shapes such as shells or spirals if these are not to hand.

Serves 4

175 g (6 oz) coloured pasta bows

salt and black pepper

166 g (5.86 oz) can tuna chunks

400 g (14 oz) can tomatoes

100 g (4 oz) button mushrooms, sliced

10 ml (2 tsp) lemon juice

15 ml (1 level tbsp) parsley, chopped

Topping

300 ml (½ pt) natural yoghurt

1 egg

50 g (2 oz) plain flour

50 g (2 oz) grated cheese (optional)

To garnish

Tomato and mushroom slices

1. Place the pasta in a casserole dish and cover with salted boiling water. Cook on HIGH power for 8 minutes. Drain and put in the base of a 1.2 lit (2 pt) souffle or casserole dish.

2. Drain the tuna chunks, then stir into the pasta with the remaining ingredients. Season to taste.

3. To make the topping, blend the yoghurt and egg in a liquidizer, then gradually blend in the flour. Season and stir in the cheese if used.

4. Pour the topping over the pasta mixture and bake in a preheated oven at 200°C, LOW power microwave for 15 minutes. Serve hot.

See photograph page 25

STUFFED MACKEREL IN APPLE JUICE

Mackerel is rich in oil, but with a delicate flavour. It does not keep well, and for this reason, in olden days it was the only fish allowed to be sold in London on a Sunday. Check that the skin is shiny and the flesh firm before buying and use on the same day.

Serves 4

4 mackerel

salt and pepper

1 eating apple, grated

15 ml (1 level tbsp) onion, finely chopped

50 g (2 oz) grated cheese

50 g (2 oz) breadcrumbs

10 ml (2 tsp) lemon juice

15 g (½ oz) butter, melted

45 ml (3 tbsp) apple juice

1. Gut the mackerel, and if wished cut off the heads. Wash thoroughly. Then dry on kitchen paper.

2. Open the mackerel up on a chopping board with the back upper most, then press firmly with the thumb all the way down the backbone. Turn over the fish and remove the backbone by slipping a knife under it. Repeat with all the fish. Season.

3. Mix together all the remaining ingredients, except for the apple juice and seasoning to taste, and use to stuff the fish. Reshape then secure with cocktail sticks.

4. Place the fish in a shallow dish and pour around the apple juice. Bake in a preheated oven at 220°C, LOW power microwave for 10 minutes or until the flesh flakes. Serve garnished with apple and parsley.

Meat

In the past, meat cooked solely by microwave has been disappointing. Its lack of colour and crispness has made it unappetizing. Although many tricks have been used (for example, microwave browning spices or colourful sauces) nothing beats the real thing. Conventional cooking gives the desired appearance, but longer cooking time can result in tough and dry meat. The combination oven marries the two methods together perfectly, to give crisp, juicy and tender meat in roughly half the time it would take conventionally. Stews and casseroles also benefit from a combination oven and even the least tender meat can be beautifully casseroled, in about an hour. The resulting casserole will have the rich flavours, generally only associated with long stove cooking. As with all casseroles, an even better flavour develops if you can resist eating it until the following day.

Recipes that call for a crisp finish, such as steak and kidney pie, cottage pie or hotpots, are also easily and quickly produced.

NB When cooking meat with a high fat content (ie, lamb, pork or duck), drain the excess fat frequently during the cooking period. If this is not done, cooking times may be longer and the meat will splatter.

BEEF WITH OLIVES

This is based on a French recipe. You will need a full blooded red wine for this and do not skimp on the brandy. There will not be much liquid left at the end so do not be alarmed, but what there is, is deliciously concentrated. Even people who are not keen on olives enjoy this dish.

Serves 4

900 g (2 lb) shin of beef

25 g (1 oz) butter

15 ml (1 tbsp) olive oil

1 large clove garlic, crushed

60 ml (4 tbsp) brandy

1 large glass red wine

2 parsley stalks, sprig of thyme, bay leaf and strip of orange rind

100 g (4 oz) black olives, stoned

1. Cut the beef into small neat cubes no larger than 2.5 cm (1 in).

2. Heat the oil and butter in a pan and fry the beef until brown on all sides. You may have to do this in two lots.

3. Add the crushed garlic.

4. Warm the brandy for 30 seconds on HIGH and pour over the meat. Set alight and shake the pan until the flames go out.

5. Add the red wine. Pour all the meat and the wine into a casserole.

6. Tie the bay leaf, orange rind, thyme and parsley together and put in the casserole.

7. Cook in the combination oven at 160°C, for 5 minutes on HIGH power and then 45 minutes on LOW power or until tender.

8. Add the olives and serve.

DAUBE

This is a wonderful casserole, based on a French recipe, very warming and filling. It uses shin of beef, a cheap cut of meat which although needing a long cooking time really has a good flavour. Normally this would take about 3 hours to cook so the time saving is considerable. It could be cooked even faster but the quality suffers. The beef is cut into slices about 1.5 cm (½ in) thick instead of cubes so each person gets a slice.
The pig's trotter can be left out but it does add to the flavour and most butchers give them away.
Remember to remove the trotter and bouquet garni before serving.

Serves 6

30 ml (4 tbsp) olive oil

700 g (1½ lb) shin beef, sliced 1.5 cm (½ in)

100 g (¼ lb) streaky bacon

150 g (6 oz) small onions

150 g (6 oz) button mushrooms

1 pigs trotter

400 g (14 oz) tin tomatoes

1 bay leaf, 3 parsley stalks and 10 cm (4 in) orange peel, all tied together

300 ml (½ pt) full bodied red wine

2.5 ml (½ tsp) salt

1. Heat the olive oil in a large frying pan and brown the beef well on both sides.

2. Place the beef into a large casserole suitable for the combination oven, then add the bacon cut into 2.5 cm (1 in) strips, the peeled onions and wiped mushrooms.

3. Tuck the trotter and bouquet garni down the side, add the tomatoes, seasoning and wine. Cover.

4. Cook on 170°C, LOW power microwave for 1 hour 10 minutes or until tender.

─── **SERVING SUGGESTION** ───
Serve with baked potatoes in their jackets or crusty bread to mop up the juices.

BEEF AU POIVRE

Steak au poivre is very popular, but is not often served at home due to the expense and worry of spoiling good steaks at a dinner party. Cooking a joint in this way is far simpler and more economical and is always a great success at our dinner parties. The joint can be prepared up to the oven stage before the guests arrive and the sauce can be made ready for reheating.

Serves 6

1.3 kg (3 lb) joint topside
30–45 ml (2–3 tbsp) whole black peppercorns
25 g (1 oz) unsalted butter
15 ml (1 tbsp) olive oil
60 ml (4 tbsp) brandy
300 ml (½ pt) double cream
salt

1. Wipe the meat. Crush the peppercorns coarsley, then press onto the surface of the meat.

2. Heat the butter and oil in a heavy based frying pan and seal the beef over a high heat, turning the joint to brown all the outside.

3. Remove from the heat. Heat the brandy until warm then pour into a ladle and set alight. Pour carefully over the beef.

4. When the flames have died down, remove the beef and roast in a preheated oven at 220°C, LOW power microwave for 30 minutes, turning occasionally.

5. Meanwhile, stir the cream into the juices in the frying pan, season with salt and reheat. Serve the meat in slices, accompanied by the sauce.

BEOUF EN CROUTE

This is the ultimate dinner party dish, yet it is so easy. All the preparation can be done in advance and at the last minute it can be cooked virtually as your guests sit down for their starter. Unfortunately beef fillet is rather expensive, however there is no waste and you only need to allow about 100–150 g (4–6 oz) per person. The time given here gives you meat which is still pink in the middle, the best way to eat fillet. If cooked for longer it dries out because there is no fat in it. We do not like pate around the meat, as in some recipes, because it makes the pastry too greasy.

Serves 6–8

900 g (2 lb) beef fillet
15 ml (1 tbsp) oil
1 small onion, finely chopped
50 g (2 oz) butter
150 g (6 oz) mushrooms, chopped
salt and pepper
450 g (1 lb) puff pastry (frozen is fine)
1 egg

1. Heat the oil in a frying pan and sear the meat on all sides so that it browns and keeps the juice in. Cool.

2. Put the onion and butter in a dish and microwave on HIGH for 3 minutes. Stir in the mushrooms and microwave on HIGH for a further 3 minutes.

3. Season well and cool.

4. Roll out the pastry to a rectangle large enough to wrap the meat completely, about 40 by 30 cm (16 by 12 in). Trim the edges.

5. Put half of the mushroom mixture down the centre of the pastry, place the fillet on it and top with the remaining mushrooms. Fold the pastry over and dampen to seal.

6. Put the roll join side down, on a greased baking dish.

7. Roll out the pastry trimmings and decorate the top with leaves. Brush twice with beaten egg.

8. Preheat the oven and bake at 220°C, LOW power microwave for 15 minutes for very rare or 20 minutes for medium rare.

--- SERVING SUGGESTION ---
Best served without a gravy but choose vegetables with a sauce to accompany it. Cauliflower cheese or broccoli with hollandaise sauce are lovely or try pommes lyonnaise.

See photograph page 66

SUET BEEF ROLL

Suet pastry has rather gone out of fashion, however now it is possible to buy vegetable suet it should come back. It makes a very substantial meal and in fact uses less fat than conventional pastry. It is also considerably quicker and easier to make.

Serves 4–6

225 g (8 oz) plain flour
80 g (3 oz) suet, shredded
5 ml (1 level tsp) salt

Filling

1 medium onion, grated
325 g (12 oz) lean minced beef
50 g (2 oz) fresh breadcrumbs
1 egg
salt and pepper
1.25 ml (¼ tsp) mixed dried herbs

1. Mix the flour, suet and salt together and add sufficient cold water to bind it into a pastry.

2. Mix all the filling ingredients together, season and check by microwaving on HIGH a small meat ball for a minute. Add any additional seasoning as necessary.

3. Roll the pastry out on a floured surface until it is 40 by 35 cm (16 × 14 in). Trim the edges and keep the trimmings.

4. Place the mince mixture down the centre of the pastry and fold the pastry over, sealing the centre and ends with a little water.

5. Place the roll join side down on a baking tray, brush with milk and decorate with leaves made from the trimmings.

6. Bake in a preheated combination oven 190°C, LOW power microwave for 25 minutes.

—— VARIATION ——
Add 15 ml (1 tbsp) of tomato puree to the meat mixture and 2.5 ml (½ tsp) mixed dried herbs to the pastry to make a herb and tomato beef roll.

COTTAGE GARDEN PIE

This is a variation on a cottage pie, altogether more interesting and certainly no longer a humble dish. It is really quickly and easily cooked in a combination oven. If you do not have any left over creamed potatoes, use potatoes in their jackets cooked in the microwave and then peeled and mashed.

Serves 4

250 g (12 oz) minced beef
1 onion, finely chopped
1 clove of garlic, crushed
100 g (4 oz) mushrooms, sliced
4 smallish tomatoes, skinned and sliced
2.5 ml (½ level tsp) marjoram
150 ml (¼ pt) beef stock (a cube will do)
15 ml (1 tbsp) tomato puree
700 g (1½ lb) potatoes, creamed
25 g (1 oz) grated cheese

1. Place the meat in a shallow casserole and microwave on HIGH for 5 minutes.

2. With a draining spoon lift out the meat.

3. Put the onion and garlic in the dish and microwave on HIGH for 4 minutes. Mix in the meat.

4. Layer the meat, mushrooms and tomatoes in a deep casserole dish.

5. Mix the herbs, stock, puree and seasoning together and pour over the meat.

6. Cover with the potatoes and sprinkle with cheese.

7. Bake in oven at 200°C, MEDIUM power for 25 minutes or at 200°C, LOW power microwave for 35 minutes.

CORNISH PASTIES

These, as the name implies, originated in Cornwall as a very easy form of packed lunch. The men who worked in the mines used to take these to work with them, giving them goodness with all the vegetables and meat they required all wrapped up in one.

Makes 6

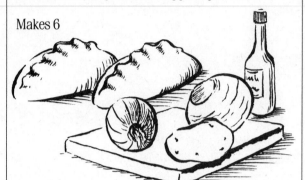

Pastry

300 g (12 oz) plain flour

75 g (3 oz) hard margarine

75 g (3 oz) lard

5 ml (1 level tsp) salt

60 ml (4 tbsp) cold water

Filling

300 g (12 oz) rump steak

150 g (6 oz) onion

200 g (8 oz) swede

200 g (8 oz) potato

15 ml (1 tbsp) Worcestershire sauce

30 ml (2 tbsp) stock

salt and pepper

1. Rub the fat into the flour and salt until it resembles breadcrumbs.

2. Add the water and knead lightly, roll out and cut into 6 × 20 cm (8 in) circles.

3. Cut the steak, swede and potato into 1.25 cm (½ in) dice. Chop the onion, mix together, season and moisten with the sauce and stock.

4. Divide the filling between the circles of pastry. Fold the circles in half and seal, moistening one edge. Crimp the edge of the pastie.

5. Bake in a preheated oven 200°C, LOW power microwave for 16–20 minutes until golden.

STEAK AND KIDNEY PIE

We have a friend married to a French girl who is a fantastic cook. Inspite of the wonderful food he gets at home he loves to come and eat steak and kidney pie at every available opportunity. This is one of the very best of the traditional English dishes. It used to be time consuming, however – not anymore!

Serves 4

30 ml (2 tbsp) oil

2 onions, sliced

750 g (1½ lb) steak and kidney

25 g (1 oz) flour

150 ml (¼ pt) beef stock

150 ml (¼ pt) red wine

15 ml (1 tbsp) tomato puree

bay leaf

seasoning

2.5 ml (½ tsp) mixed dried herbs

225 g (8 oz) puff pastry

egg for glazing

1. Place the oil in a casserole suitable for the combination oven and add the onions and meat. Microwave on HIGH for 5 minutes, stirring 2 or 3 times.

2. Stir in the flour then gradually add the liquids, bay leaf, seasoning and herbs.

3. Cover the casserole and cook at 175°C, 5 minutes HIGH power, stir then 20 minutes on LOW power, stir again then another 20 minutes on LOW power. Check to see if tender; if not cook a little longer. Leave to cool. Place the meat in a pie dish.

5. Roll the pastry out 2.5 cm (1 in) larger than the top of the dish, cut 1.2 cm (½ in) strip from around the edge. Place on the dampened rim of the dish.

6. Dampen the pastry edges with water and place on top of the pie. Trim, knock up the edges and scallop.

7. Roll out the pastry trimmings into leaves and decorate the pie. Brush twice with egg.

8. Bake in a preheated oven 200°C, HIGH power microwave for 5 minutes, then LOW power for 10–15 minutes until golden brown.

See photograph page 68

MEAT LOAF WITH BARBECUE SAUCE

Meat loaves have a bad name, as they smack of leftovers and frugal meals. This one is different, it is still economical but it is definitely delicious, and with its glowing sauce coat, looks good. Normally a meat loaf takes an hour or so to cook; now with your combination oven this is reduced to 15 minutes.

Serves 4

15 ml (1 tbsp) sunflower oil
small onion, finely chopped
1 stick of celery, finely chopped
1 small carrot, finely grated
50 g (2 oz) breadcrumbs
450 g (1 lb) lean mince
1 small egg
salt and pepper
30 ml (2 tbsp) tomato sauce
15 ml (1 tbsp) Worcestershire sauce

Sauce

15 ml (1 tbsp) wine vinegar
15 ml (1 tbsp) brown sugar
5 ml (1 tsp) mustard
45 ml (3 tbsp) tomato sauce

1. Put the oil and onion in a mixing bowl and microwave on HIGH for 3 minutes.

2. Add all the other ingredients and mix well. A fork is helpful to break up the meat.

3. Pile the mixture into a dish and make into a loaf shape.

4. Mix the sauce ingredients together and spread over the loaf. Bake in a preheated oven at 200°C, MEDIUM power microwave for 16 minutes or LOW power for 25 minutes.

5. Leave to cool before lifting the meat loaf out of the dish.

—— SERVING SUGGESTION ——
Serve cold with jacket potatoes and salad.

CROWN ROAST OF LAMB

If a little warning is given, most butchers will be happy to prepare a crown roast for you. The meat on a crown roast cooked conventionally can often dry out before the stuffing is cooked – the combination oven solves this problem.

Serves 6

2 joints best end of neck of lamb
100 g (4 oz) fresh breadcrumbs
2 dessert apples, cored and chopped
2 sticks celery, chopped
1 small onion, peeled and chopped
15 ml (1 level tbsp) parsley, chopped
50 g (2 oz) raisins
1 egg
30 ml (2 tbsp) milk
salt and pepper
oil

1. Ask your butcher to prepare the crown roast, or if this is not possible, ask him to chine the joints and remove any surplus fat from around the bones, so that they protrude.

2. Using string and a trussing needle, sew the joints together, back to back to form the crown. Place in a roasting dish.

3. Mix together all the remaining ingredients, except for the oil, binding the mixture with the egg and milk. Pack into the centre of the crown and cover the stuffing with oiled grease-proof paper.

4. Brush the outside of the joint with the oil and cook at 200°C, LOW power microwave for 50 minutes. Serve with cutlet frills on each bone tip.

—— VARIATION ——
Other stuffings can be used for this joint and one of our favourites is sausagemeat, breadcrumbs, onion and cranberry sauce.

BARBECUED LEG OF LAMB

This is an unusual way of serving lamb but it is delicious and looks lovely, quite suitable for a dinner party with creamed potatoes and green vegetables. It is a delight to carve. Ask your butcher to bone the lamb for you and use the bones for the stock. Trim the leg of most of the fat. It should be pink still in the centre when cooked.

Serves 6

1.6–1.8 kg (3½–4 lb) leg of lamb, boned
30 ml (2 level tbsp) flour

Spicy mixture

5 ml (1 level tsp) dry mustard
5 ml (1 level tsp) sugar
5 ml (1 level tsp) black pepper
5 ml (1 level tsp) ground ginger
2 cloves of garlic, crushed

Stock

1 onion, chopped
25 g (1 oz) dripping or fat
lamb bones
5 ml (1 level tsp) cornflour

Barbecue sauce mixture

30 ml (2 tbsp) tomato sauce
30 ml (2 tbsp) mushroom ketchup
30 ml (2 tbsp) Worcestershire sauce
30 ml (2 tbsp) spicy fruit sauce
5 ml (1 tsp) Tabasco sauce
5 ml (1 tsp) vinegar

1. Mix all the spice ingredients together and coat the lamb and the inside of the leg with them. Tie the joint and leave for 24 hours if possible, then dust with the 30 ml (2 level tbsp) flour.

2. Fry the onion in the fat until well browned, add the bones and brown those. Add 1 pint of water and simmer for 45 minutes. Use a saucepan on the hob.

3. Strain the stock and then reduce to 275 ml (½ pt) by rapid boiling, cool and skim.

4. Mix the barbecue sauce mixture together, and divide into 2.

5. Add half to the reduced stock and use the other half to cover the joint.

6. Place the lamb on a rack and cook at 200°C, LOW power microwave for 50 minutes turning once.

7. Slake the cornflour with a little water, add to the barbecue sauce mixture in a jug and bring to the boil. Boil for 3 minutes on HIGH power until thick.

8. Carve the meat at the table and pass the sauce separately.

LAMB IN BURGUNDY

This is a recipe that we have been using for sometime at the cookery school. Lamb stews often tend to be a bit homely, but this one is definitely not. It has a lovely glowing red sauce, tastes delicious and is really quite easy. You could cook it faster but the result does suffer. By adding the onions later they keep their shape and look much better. You could saute the meat in the microwave but we prefer to do it over a high heat on the hob.

Serves 4

25 g (1 oz) butter

30 ml (2 tbsp) olive oil

150 g (6 oz) button onions or small onions cut in half

700 g (1½ lb) lamb cut into 3 cm (1¼ in) cubes (use lean leg meat)

35 g (1½ oz) flour

15 ml (1 tbsp) tomato puree

280 ml (½ pt) burgundy or full bodied red wine

bay leaf

2.5 ml (½ tsp) thyme

2.5 ml (½ tsp) marjoram

150 g (6 oz) button mushrooms

1. Heat the butter and olive oil in a large frying pan and fry the onions until glazed all over, 2–3 minutes. Remove.

2. Add the meat to the frying pan half at a time and fry until sealed on all sides. Remove from the pan and put in a casserole.

3. Add the flour to the pan, stir round, remove from the heat, add the tomato puree and gradually the wine. Stir well.

4. Add the herbs, seasonings and mushrooms. Pour over the meat and mix.

5. Cook at 170°C, HIGH power microwave for 5 minutes then 15 minutes LOW power. Stir.

6. Add the onions. Cook at 170°C, LOW power microwave for 20 minutes or until the meat is tender.

See photograph page 66

STUFFED SHOULDER OF LAMB

A shoulder of lamb is a relatively inexpensive joint. It is however a very awkward shape and is impossible to carve. By boning and stuffing it you have a neat easily carved joint which will easily serve 8. It is not difficult to bone but your butcher should do it for you if you ask. Keep the bones, they can be simmered to make the gravy. Choose one of the 2 stuffing recipes; the methods are the same.

Serves 8

1.75 kg (approx 4 lb) shoulder lamb, boned (weight before boning)

25 g (1 oz) butter

salt and pepper

Herb stuffing

25 g (1 oz) butter

1 medium onion, finely chopped

30 ml (2 level tbsp) parsley, chopped

5 ml (1 level tsp) rosemary

2.5 ml (½ tsp) mixed herbs

50 g (2 oz) fresh breadcrumbs

1 egg

salt and pepper

Apple stuffing

25 g (1 oz) butter

1 medium onion, finely chopped

50 g (2 oz) fresh breadcrumbs

225 g (8 oz) pork, minced

100 g (4 oz) grated apple

15 ml (1 level tbsp) parsley, chopped

1 egg

salt and pepper

1. Fry the onion in butter until soft then add all the remaining stuffing ingredients and mix well.

2. Spread the stuffing over the meat where the bone was. Roll up the joint and tie with string.

3. Put the joint in a roasting dish, spread with butter and roast at 200°C, LOW power microwave for 45 minutes, turning once. If using the apple stuffing add on 5 minutes.

4. Serve with gravy made from bone stock and meat juices from the roasting dish.

LAMB SQUAB PIE

There are many variations to this recipe, depending on which part of the country you come from. Originally it contained 'squabs' which is an old word for pigeons, but now most recipes are purely lamb.

Serves 4

Pastry

150 g (6 oz) plain flour

pinch of salt

75 g (3 oz) margarine or lard and margarine

30 ml (2 tbsp) water

Filling

4 lamb chops

15 g (½ oz) lard

225 g (8 oz) cooking apples, peeled, cored and sliced

1 onion, peeled and sliced

salt and pepper

300 ml (½ pt) chicken or lamb stock

To glaze

milk or beaten egg

1. Sieve the flour and salt into a bowl, then rub in the fat until the mixture resembles fine breadcrumbs. Stir in the water, then knead lightly to form a soft dough. Set aside.

2. Melt the lard in a frying pan and quickly fry the chops on both sides.

3. Place half the apples and onions in the base of a 900 ml (1½ pt) pie dish, cover with the chops, then the remaining apple and onion. Add a little seasoning to the stock, then pour over.

4. Roll out the pastry on a floured surface. Dampen the edge of the dish, place a strip of pastry around the top, dampen again and cover with the pastry lid and trim.

5. Seal the edges and make a whole in the centre. Decorate with pastry leaves, then brush with milk or egg. Bake in a preheated oven at 200°C, LOW power microwave for 20–25 minutes or until golden brown.

LANCASHIRE HOTPOT

This is a very old dish and there are lots of variations to the recipe. Traditionally, when they were cheap, a layer of oysters were put beneath the potato topping.

Serves 4

8 middle neck lamb chops

450 g (1 lb) potatoes

1 onion, peeled and sliced

1 stick celery, sliced

1 leek, sliced

2.5 ml (½ tsp) mixed herbs

salt and pepper

melted lard or dripping

1. Bone the chops and trim off any extra fat. Cover the bones with water and simmer on the hob or in the microwave on MEDIUM for ½ hour, then strain off 300 ml (½ pt) of stock.

2. Peel and thinly slice the potatoes then use half to cover the base of a deep casserole dish.

3. Mix the remaining vegetables together, place half over the potatoes, cover with the lamb, then top with the remaining mixed vegetables. Arrange the potato slices on top.

4. Add the herbs and seasoning to the stock and pour over the casserole. Cover and cook in a preheated oven at 180°C, LOW power microwave for 30 minutes.

5. Remove the lid, brush the potatoes with a little melted lard or dripping and continue cooking at LOW power microwave for a further 30 minutes, turning the temperature up to 190°C to brown the potatoes.

——— COOK'S TIP ———
Very cheap frozen New Zealand lamb cutlets can be used for this recipe.

MOUSSAKA

A spicy Mediterranean dish which must summon up memories of summer holidays in Greece. This is a traditional recipe with a baked custard topping. Even with the combination oven, this recipe takes a while to prepare, but the result is well worth the trouble.

Serves 4

3 aubergines

salt and black pepper

vegetable or olive oil

2 large onions, sliced

450 g (1 lb) minced lamb

400 g (14 oz) can tomatoes

1 chicken stock cube

2.5 ml (½ tsp) basil

2.5 ml (½ tsp) cinnamon

Topping

300 ml (½ pt) milk

2 eggs

25 g (1 oz) plain flour

1. Slice the aubergines and sprinkle with salt then leave to stand for ½ hour. Rinse in cold water and dry thoroughly on kitchen paper.

2. Heat some oil in a large frying pan and quickly fry the aubergines on both sides. Drain on kitchen paper.

3. Place 15 ml (1 tbsp) oil in a casserole dish and stir in the onion and minced lamb. Cook on HIGH power in the microwave for 5 minutes, stirring occasionally. Drain off any excess oil.

4. Add the tinned tomatoes to the mince, breaking up with a fork. Sprinkle in the stock cube, basil and cinnamon and season to taste.

5. Lightly grease a 20–25 cm (8–9 in) deep square dish. Cover the base with a layer of aubergines then top with meat mixture. Repeat until all the ingredients are used up.

6. To make the topping, place the milk and egg in a liquidizer and puree until smooth. Blend in the flour. Pour into a bowl or jug and heat on HIGH power in the microwave for 3–4 minutes, stirring regularly, until the custard just begins to thicken. Season.

7. Pour over the meat and aubergines and bake in a preheated oven at 200°C, LOW power microwave for 20 minutes. Usually served hot, but also delicious cold.

SATE PORK

This is an Indonesian recipe and if you are ever visiting the country a meal at an Indonesian restaurant is something not to be missed.

Serves 6

900 g (2 lb) lean pork, cut into cubes

175 g (6 oz) salted peanuts

2 cloves garlic, crushed

1 large onion, chopped

60 ml (4 tbsp) soy sauce

45 ml (3 tbsp) lemon juice

15 ml (1 tbsp) chilli sauce

25 g (1 oz) soft brown sugar

black pepper

450 ml (¾ pt) chicken stock

1. Thread the pork loosely onto wooden kebab sticks, then place in a shallow dish.

2. Place all the remaining ingredients in a liquidizer and blend until smooth.

3. Pour about half the sauce over the pork (the remaining can be heated up and served in a sauce boat), and cook in a preheated oven at 220°C, LOW power microwave for 20–25 minutes.

—— SERVING SUGGESTION ——
This goes well with rice and a green salad. If wooden kebab sticks cannot be found, serve the pork in the sauce casserole style.

See photograph page 67

STUFFED RIB OF PORK

A joint is always a success at a dinner party, and this one is extra special. We were served this by a great friend and managed to steal and adapt her recipe! The butcher will usually be happy to prepare the joint for you, ready for stuffing, but do make sure he keeps the rib flat and that he does not cut all the way through the meat. The finished result should look like a sandwich with a flat layer of crackling and meat on top, then the filling and another layer of meat.

Serves 6

1.5 kg (3½ lb) rib of pork (weight after boning)
25 g (1 oz) butter
100 g (4 oz) button mushrooms, chopped
75 g (3 oz) smoked ham, chopped
100 g (4 oz) minced pork
50 g (2 oz) fresh breadcrumbs
15 ml (1 level tbsp) parsley, chopped
5 ml (1 level tsp) dried sage
60 ml (4 tbsp) double cream
salt and freshly ground black pepper

Gravy

10 ml (2 level tsp) plain flour
300 ml (½ pt) chicken stock
soy sauce

1. Bone the meat with a sharp knife, if the butcher has not already done this, and score the crackling. Cut crossways, almost through the meat and open it up.

2. Melt the butter in a bowl on HIGH power for 1 minute then stir in the mushrooms and ham. Return to the oven and cook on HIGH power for 2 minutes. Stir in the remaining ingredients and season.

3. Spread the stuffing evenly over one side of the meat, then fold over the top. If possible, stitch the open sides with a trussing needle and string to keep in the filling. Alternatively secure with cocktail sticks, but this method is not as effective.

4. Place the meat in a roasting dish and rub salt into the crackling. Cook in a preheated oven at 200°C, LOW power microwave for 40–45 minutes or until the juices run clear when a skewer is inserted in the meat.

5. To make the gravy, strain 15 ml (1 tbsp) of the juices from the roasting dish into a bowl and stir in the flour. Blend in the stock and a little soy sauce to taste. Return to the microwave on HIGH power for 3–4 minutes, whisking thoroughly on completion.

6. Remove the string or cocktail stick from the meat and serve in fairly thick slices, accompanied by the gravy.

—— **VARIATION** ——
A stuffing made up of apples, cheese and breadcrumbs could be used with a cider gravy.

PORK CHOPS WITH APPLE AND CIDER CREAM SAUCE

Chops are often disappointing as they tend to dry out and toughen when cooked. But they are a good standby and very useful to serve, portion control is easy, and you always know that if you have counted right you will not have to say you are on a diet. This recipe uses the combination method of cooking for the chops and the microwave only for the sauce and the result will not be disappointing; the chops will be tender and moist.

Serves 4

4 pork chops about 175 g (6 oz) each
2 Coxs apples, cored, cut into 8ths
15 ml (1 level tbsp) flour
150 ml (¼ pt) cider
150 ml (¼ pt) double cream
seasoning

1. Remove the rind from the chops, put in a dish in a single layer. Bake in a pre-heated oven at 220°C, LOW power microwave for 12 minutes. Remove and put on a serving platter.

2. Toss the apples in the meat juices and cook at 220°C, LOW power microwave for 6 minutes.

3. Remove the apples with a draining spoon and scatter over the chops.

4. Stir the flour into the meat juices and gradually add the cider.

5. Microwave the sauce on HIGH power for 3 minutes, stirring well once or twice until thickened and smooth.

6. Stir in the cream and season to taste, microwave on HIGH for 30 seconds and pour over the chops.

HERB STUFFED FILLET OF PORK WITH SAUCE

This is one of those great recipes that can be made in advance, cooked, sliced and then arranged on a serving dish. Reheat in the microwave just before serving. An ideal dish for entertaining.

Serves 8

Stuffing

4 pork fillets approximately 1 kg (2 lb)
1 large onion, finely chopped
1 clove of garlic, crushed
150 g (6 oz) minced pork
100 g (4 oz) breadcrumbs
1 egg
salt and pepper
50 g (2 oz) apricots, soaked and chopped
handful of parsley, chopped
5 ml (1 level tsp) fresh thyme, chopped
5 ml (1 level tsp) fresh sage, chopped

Sauce

200 ml (⅓ pt) white wine
15 ml (1 tbsp) tomato puree
30 ml (2 tbsp) apple jelly
10 ml (2 level tsp) arrow root

1. Cut each fillet lengthways almost in half and open up like a book. Beat out the pork with a mallet or rolling pin.

2. Mix all the stuffing ingredients together and bind with the egg. Divide into 4 pieces.

3. Place the stuffing on the fillets and roll each one up, to make a long narrow cylinder, then tie with string. Put in a baking dish.

4. Cook in a preheated oven at 200°C, LOW power microwave for 15 minutes.

5. Roll the meat in the juices and set aside.

6. Gradually add the wine to the meat juices, the puree and apple jelly, and season to taste. Mix the arrowroot with a little of the liquid, add to the rest and microwave on HIGH for 4 minutes or until thick, stirring once or twice.

7. Slice the meat into 1.5 cm (½ in) slices and arrange on a plate. Garnish with parsley and a little sauce.

SPARE RIBS

These are a great favourite with most people – it must be the picking up and eating with the fingers that appeals. In the past we have found it quite difficult to get them tender without drying them out too much. The combination oven changes all that. If you have time, marinade them for a couple of hours.

Serves 4

1 kg (2 lb) spare ribs
90 ml (6 tbsp) tomato sauce
30 ml (2 tbsp) vinegar
15 ml (1 level tbsp) sugar
5 ml (1 tsp) mustard
30 ml (2 tbsp) Worcestershire sauce
60 ml (4 tbsp) soy sauce

1. Cut the spare ribs so they are individual bones.

2. Combine the sauce ingredients and pour over the ribs. Mix well and leave for a couple of hours.

3. Bake at 200°C, LOW power microwave for 35 minutes turning them in the sauce once.

4. Remove the ribs onto a serving plate and if necessary reduce the sauce to thicken on HIGH power.

See photograph page 67

CASSOULET

This is a variation of a French peasant dish, is very substantial and can easily be extended to feed a large party. It usually involves cooking for hours but this recipe has part of it cooked in advance and then a final cooking in the combination oven after it has been assembled.

Serves 6–8

450 g (1 lb) haricot beans soaked overnight

1 large onion, chopped

at least 4 cloves of garlic, sliced

350 g (12 oz) slice of gammon

1 bay leaf, sprig of thyme and parsley stalks or a bouquet garni

2 duck portions

450 g (1 lb) belly pork

250 g (½ lb) garlic sausage in a piece

400 g (14 oz) tin tomatoes

seasoning

75 g (3 oz) breadcrumbs

1. Drain the beans and put them in a large pan with the onion, garlic, gammon and bouquet garni, cover with water, bring to the boil and simmer for 1½ hours (or pressure cook for 35 minutes). It is no quicker in a microwave.

2. Remove the bacon and drain the beans, keeping the liquid.

3. Put the duck and pork in a roasting dish and roast in a preheated oven at 200°C, LOW power microwave for 30 minutes.

4. Cut the duck, pork bacon and sausage into pieces. Drain the tomatoes.

5. In a large deep casserole layer the beans, meat and tomatoes, seasoning each layer and starting and ending with the beans. Pour in enough of the bean liquid to come ¾ of the way up the casserole.

6. Cover with the breadcrumbs and bake at 180°C, LOW power microwave for 50 minutes or until golden on the top.

GLAZED GAMMON

For big parties or at holiday time, nothing could be better than a home cooked joint of gammon. By using the combination oven a glazed joint can be cooked in the minimum time and with no effort at all – well worth trying.

Serves 12

approximately 2.2 kg (5 lb) joint boned gammon

600 ml (1 pt) cider

brown sugar

1. Soak the gammon in cold water for at least 3 hours or preferably overnight. Change the water several times.

2. Place the gammon in a deep casserole dish and pour over the cider. Cover and cook in a preheated oven at 190°C, LOW power microwave for 1¼ hours.

3. Drain and remove the skin from the gammon. Score the fat with a sharp knife in a diamond pattern and pat with brown sugar. Return to the oven in an open dish at 200°C, LOW power microwave for a further 15 minutes. Leave to cool.

—— **VARIATION** ——
The joint can be studded with cloves when the sugar is added or glazed with honey.

Haddock and prawn cobbler (page 30); Tomato and herb bread (page 90); Plaice filo rolls (page 16).

OVERLEAF
Left to right: Tandoori chicken (page 56); Chicken marsala (page 54); Pigeon with redcurrant sauce (page 61); Pommes lyonnaise (page 69).

BLACKEYED BEAN AND BACON HOTPOT

This is an incredibly economical dish as the rolled forehock is one of the cheapest cuts of meat. It was recommended by our butcher one day when we were short of ideas and cash, and we have now slipped it into all sorts of different recipes. The sweetness of the parsnip topping goes very well with the bacon and beans and makes a refreshing change from traditional hotpots.

Serves 4

125 g (4 oz) blackeyed beans
450 g (1 lb) rolled forehock (cut into 4 slices)
1 onion, peeled and chopped
425 g (15 oz) tin of tomatoes
150 ml (¼ pt) water
2.5 ml (½ tsp) thyme
2.5 ml (½ tsp) oregano
freshly ground black pepper
450 g (1 lb) parsnips
15 ml (1 tbsp) oil

1. Rinse the beans then soak overnight in water. Drain.

2. Place the sliced forehock in a 1.8 lit (3 pt) casserole dish, then cover with the beans, onion, tomatoes, water, herbs and pepper. Stir.

3. Peel the parsnips and slice thinly. Place in a bowl with the oil and toss with a spoon until well coated. Layer over the bean mixture.

4. Cover and cook at 180°C, LOW power microwave for 20 minutes, then uncover and cook at LOW power for a further 20 minutes. Brush the top with a little

more oil if necessary, and turn up the temperature a little towards the end of the cooking time if a crisper topping is desired.

—————— COOK'S TIP ——————
If, like us you forget to soak the beans overnight, place them in a saucepan cover with cold water and bring to the boil. Boil for 2–3 minutes then leave to stand for a couple of hours.

SAUSAGE PLAIT

This is a good standby, it is very economical to make and the ingredients can be varied quite considerably. Try putting whole hard boiled eggs into the middle and take out on a lovely sunny day's picnic.

Serves 4

215 g (7½ oz) packet puff pastry
225 g (8 oz) low fat pork sausage meat
1 onion, chopped
50 g (2 oz) cheese, grated
50 g (2 oz) mushrooms, sliced
45 ml (3 tbsp) tomato chutney
15 ml (1 tbsp) Worcestershire sauce
pinch mixed herbs
salt and pepper
1 egg, lightly beaten

1. Roll out the pastry to an oblong 35×30 cm (14×12 in).

2. Mix together the remaining ingredients, reserving a little of the egg for glazing. Spoon down the centre third of the pastry leaving a margin at the top and bottom.

3. Using a sharp knife cut diagonal slits every 1 cm (½ in) down each side of the pastry.

4. Brush the edges with egg, fold in the top and bottom, then plait the strips over the filling. Lift onto a baking sheet and brush with remaining egg. Bake in the oven at 220°C, HIGH power microwave for 5 minutes, then LOW power for a further 10–15 minutes.

Onions stuffed with raisins and oregano (page 78); Rabbit tagine with prunes (page 63); Sausage plait (page 49).

See photograph page 48

SAUSAGE STEW WITH CRISPY DUMPLINGS

This is very much a one dish meal with vegetables, meat and carbohydrates all in the same pot. It always disappears remarkably quickly, and is especially popular with children.

Serves 4

30 ml (2 tbsp) oil
2 onions, sliced
2 carrots, thinly sliced
2 sticks celery, sliced
2 rashers bacon in 1.2 cm (½ in) strips
450 g (1 lb) pork sausages
1 chicken stock cube
pinch mixed herbs
150 g (6 oz) self raising flour
75 g (3 oz) suet, shredded
5 ml (1 level tsp) salt

1. Put the oil and onions in a casserole and microwave on HIGH for 3 minutes.

2. Add the carrots and microwave on HIGH for a further 3 minutes.

3. Add the bacon, celery, sausages cut into 3, stock cube and 1 lit (1½ pt) boiling water and stir.

4. Cover and cook in an oven at 200°C, LOW power microwave for 20 minutes.

5. Mix together the flour, suet and salt, adding sufficient cold water to make it into a dry dough. Roll into 8 balls.

6. Add the dumplings to the casserole, baste them and cover. Cook on 200°C, LOW power microwave for 10 minutes.

7. Remove the lid and cook for a further 10 minutes at 200°C, no microwave. If they are not brown on top just leave the oven on with no microwave to finish off.

LIVER HOTPOT

The word 'offal' has a rather unappetising ring to it, which is not surprising as it originated from 'off falls' – in other words, bits that are left over after a carcass has been jointed! Liver is, however, one of the most nutritious meats being high in minerals and vitamins and having a delicious flavour if carefully cooked. It is also extremely cheap. This is a really tasty and economical hotpot.

Serves 4

450 g (1 lb) lambs liver, sliced
15 ml (1 tbsp) seasonal flour
1 onion, peeled and sliced
2 carrots, peeled and sliced
1 turnip, peeled and chopped
2 sticks celery, sliced
450 g (1 lb) potatoes, peeled and thinly sliced
salt and black pepper
350 ml (12 fl oz) hot chicken or lamb stock
lard or dripping

1. Dip the liver in seasoned flour. Mix together the onion, carrot, turnip and celery.

2. Place a layer of mixed vegetables in the base of a deep casserole dish, cover with liver, then repeat the layers.

3. Arrange the potatoes on the top. Add a little seasoning to the stock, then pour over the hotpot. Cover and cook in a preheated oven at 180°C, LOW power microwave for 30 minutes. Remove the lid, brush with melted fat and return to the oven at LOW power for a further 20 minutes, turning up the temperature to 190°C.

STUFFED LIVER

Bacon and liver always go well together, and with the breadcrumb stuffing, this makes a substantial dish. Calves liver is very tender and really melts in the mouth, but lambs liver, which is more economical is a good substitute.

Serves 4

450 g (1 lb) calves or lambs liver, sliced

125 g (4 oz) fresh breadcrumbs

1 onion, peeled and finely chopped

5 ml (1 level tsp) sage

15 ml (1 level tbsp) parsley, chopped

30 ml (2 tbsp) tomato ketchup

salt and black pepper

175 g (6 oz) smoked streaky bacon

300 ml (½ pt) hot chicken stock

1. Arrange the liver in a single layer in a shallow dish.

2. Mix together the breadcrumbs, onion, sage, parsley, tomato ketchup and seasoning. Spread over the liver.

3. Derind the bacon, then use to cover the breadcrumbs. Pour over the stock and cook in a preheated oven at 220°C, LOW power microwave for 20 minutes.

—— SERVING SUGGESTION ——
A packet of sage and onion stuffing mix can be used in place of the breadcrumbs stuffing with the recommended amount of liquid.

HEART WITH PEPPERS

Offal is very underused these days which is a shame because it is cheap and nutritious. This recipe combines it with cumin and peppers. It looks lovely and tastes delicious served with rice.

Serves 4

450 g (1 lb) ox or pigs heart, thinly sliced

15 ml (1 tbsp) oil

225 g (½ lb) onions, sliced

225 g (½ lb) mixed peppers, sliced (red, green, yellow)

10 ml (2 level tsp) cumin

2.5 ml (½ tsp) chilli

400 g (14 oz) tin of tomatoes

salt and pepper

1. Place the sliced heart and oil in a casserole, stir and microwave on HIGH for 3 minutes.

2. Add the onions and microwave on HIGH for 3 minutes.

3. Stir in the peppers and spices and the tomatoes and cook at 170°C, LOW power microwave for 40 minutes or until tender. Stir once or twice.

4. Check the seasoning as it will need salt.

See photograph page 68

Poultry and Game

The best method of roasting poultry and game is undoubtably
the combination system. Whilst giving a traditional brown and crisp appearance
the flesh remains deliciously moist and succulent. Even a frozen chicken,
notorious for its lack of flavour, benefits greatly from this method.
It is best to start cooking birds, breast side down and turn halfway through the
cooking time. For game birds a knob of butter inside will help to keep them moist.
Normally, when portions of poultry are cooked the meat has a tendency to dry out
before the outside is crisp, but this is now no longer the case. Duck in particular
benefits from combination cooking. Much of the unwanted fat drains out leaving
tender and moist, but not greasy meat.

TARRAGON CHICKEN

This is wonderful – chicken will never taste the same after you have tried it. Serve with a green salad and lovely fresh bread to mop up the juices. The chicken is white and succulent with a crisp skin.

Serves 4

1 chicken cut into 10

Marinade

90 ml (6 tbsp) sunflower oil

30 ml (2 tbsp) wine vinegar

30 ml (2 tbsp) lemon juice

2 cloves of garlic, crushed

15 ml (1 level tbsp) fresh tarragon or 7.5 ml (½ level tsp) of dried tarragon

freshly ground black pepper

1. Combine all the marinade ingredients. Put the chicken in the marinade and cover. Marinade for at least 2 hours, preferably overnight.

2. Grill on high, under a preheated grill, HIGH power microwave for 6 minutes, turn and grill on LOW power microwave for 6 minutes. If your oven does not have a grill cook in a preheated oven at 220°C, HIGH power microwave for 6 minutes, turn and cook for 8 minutes LOW power.

3. Serve garnished with fresh tarragon.

CHICKEN AND OLIVES EN CROUTE

This is a delicious dinner party dish to serve, accompanied by fresh vegetables or a salad. The pastry is light and golden and the combination of ingredients in the filling unusual. It has the advantage of being able to be prepared in advance and cooked at the last minute. The pastry parcels freeze well, but should be defrosted completely before cooking.

Serves 4

375 g (13 oz) puff pastry

100 g (4 oz) stuffed olives, sliced

100 g (4 oz) Gouda cheese, grated

100 g (4 oz) smoked bacon, chopped

30 ml (2 tbsp) white wine or Martini

pinch of rosemary

salt and black pepper

4 small boned chicken breasts

To glaze

beaten egg or milk

1. Roll out the pastry to a large square and cut into 4 small squares, 20 cm (8 in) wide.

2. Mix together the olives, cheese, bacon, wine and rosemary and season to taste.

3. Place a spoon full of filling on a pastry square, top with a chicken breast, then cover with another spoon of filling. Repeat with all the squares.

4. Brush the edges of the squares with egg or milk, then fold each up like a parcel.

5. Place, cut side down on a baking dish and brush with more egg or milk. Use any pastry trimmings to decorate. Bake in a preheated oven at 200°C, LOW power microwave for 20–25 minutes.

—— COOK'S TIP ——
Cooked chicken breast can be used in place of raw, but cook on a higher temperature for a slightly shorter time.

CHICKEN MARSALA

This is another delicious boned and stuffed recipe made doubly good by the addition of marsala to the sauce. Do not worry if you do not have any marsala – a medium to sweet sherry will do instead.
If you want to make this in advance, bone the chicken and freeze it for later. Mix up the stuffing, but do not stuff the bird until just before you are going to cook it.

Serves 6

1½–2 kg (3½–4½ lb) fresh chicken

Stuffing

125 g (4 oz) smooth liver pate

50 g (2 oz) cooked ham, chopped

125 g (4 oz) white breadcrumbs

15 ml (1 level tbsp) parsley, chopped

1 small onion, chopped

salt and pepper

1 small egg

1 clove garlic, crushed

1.25 ml (¼ tsp) ground nutmeg

Marsala sauce

25 g (1 oz) butter

1 small onion, finely chopped

25 g (1 oz) flour

150 ml (5 fl oz) marsala

150 ml (5 fl oz) chicken stock

110 g (4 oz) button mushrooms, sliced finely

salt and black pepper

1. Bone the chicken, then spread out the flesh on a board and season the inside with salt and pepper. (see boned stuffed turkey recipe, page 58).

2. Mix together all the stuffing ingredients, binding with the egg, then spoon down the centre of the chicken.

3. Fold over the edges of the chicken overlapping the wing edges and folding up the ends to form a neat shape. Sew together with a trussing needle and string or secure with cocktail sticks.

4. Place the breast side down in a high-sided roasting dish and brush with a little oil. Cook at 200°C, LOW power microwave for 40 minutes, turning once and draining the juices halfway through the cooking time.

To make the sauce

1. Melt the butter in a jug on HIGH power for 1 minute.

2. Add the onion and microwave and cook on HIGH power for 3 minutes.

3. Stir in the flour and microwave on HIGH for 30 seconds. Gradually add the liquid and beat well.

4. Add the mushrooms and cook on HIGH for 3 minutes. Stir well, season and cook for a further 2 minutes on HIGH or until thick and the mushrooms are cooked. Serve the chicken cut into slices, accompanied by the Marsala sauce.

See photograph page 46

CHICKEN AND LEEK PIE

A good, plain recipe which can be cooked using raw or cooked chicken. We have deliberately kept the recipe simple, but do feel free to add herbs of your own choice, a dash of wine or cream, or a variety of other vegetables. There is certainly plenty of scope here, but this is a good basic pie to start with, so that cooking times can be worked out.

Serves 4

Pastry

150 g (6 oz) plain flour

pinch of salt

75 g (3 oz) margarine or margarine and lard

30 ml (2 tbsp) water

Filling

450 g (1 lb) leeks (350 g [12 oz] when washed and trimmed)

350 g (12 oz) raw chicken meat, roughly chopped

1 small onion

15 ml (1 level tbsp) cornflour

300 ml (½ pt) chicken stock

salt and pepper

milk or beaten egg to glaze

1. To make the pastry, sieve the flour and salt into a bowl and rub in the fat.

2. Add the water and mix with a knife, then knead with fingers to a soft dough. Set aside.

3. Slice the leeks then layer with the chicken and onion in a 900 ml (1½ pt) pie dish. Blend the cornflour with a little of the stock, then add to the pie with the remaining stock.

4. Roll out the pastry on a floured surface. Brush the edge of the pie dish with milk or beaten egg. Place a strip of pastry around the edge of the dish, dampen then cover with the pastry lid. Trim the edges then seal.

5. Make a hole in the centre of the pie, brush with the milk or egg, then decorate with leaves made from the pastry trimmings.

6. Bake in a preheated oven at 190°C, LOW power microwave for 30 minutes.

—— **VARIATION** ——

Cooked chicken meat can be used instead of raw, in which case raise the oven temperature to 200°C and cook for 20 minutes. Courgettes can be used instead of leeks.

FONTSAINTE CHICKEN

This recipe was devised whilst staying on the Fontsainte vineyard in the South of France. As wine and brandy are freely available during the 'vindage' we ended up as well marinaded as the chicken! It can be more economical to buy a whole chicken for this recipe and quarter or joint it yourself.

Serves 4

50 g (2 oz) smoked streaky bacon, chopped

1 onion, peeled and chopped

1 clove garlic, crushed

125 g (4 oz) button mushrooms, sliced

4 tomatoes, skinned and sliced

2.5 ml (½ tsp) tarragon

salt and pepper

150 ml (¼ pt) red wine

60 ml (4 tbsp) brandy

4 chicken portions

5 ml (1 level tsp) cornflour

150 ml (¼ pt) double cream

1. Place the bacon, onion and garlic in a shallow ovenproof dish and microwave on HIGH power for 4 minutes.

2. Add the mushrooms, tomatoes, seasoning and tarragon, then stir in over the wine and brandy.

3. Season the chicken portions, then place on top of the sauce mixture. Cook in a preheated oven at 220°C, LOW power microwave for 20–25 minutes, turning the chicken occasionally.

4. Remove the chicken and place on a warm serving dish. Blend the cornflour with a little water and stir into the sauce with the cream. Return to the oven on HIGH power for 2–3 minutes. Pour the sauce over the chicken and serve, perhaps with a savoury rice and a salad.

TANDOORI CHICKEN

This is a spicy recipe, with a good 'kick' to it, but is not unbearably hot. When marinading overnight, make sure that it is well covered or the flavour will taint other foods!

Serves 4

150 ml (¼ pt) natural yoghurt
grated rind and juice of 1 lemon
5 ml (1 level tsp) ground ginger
5 ml (1 level tsp) chilli powder
5 ml (1 level tsp) ground coriander
2.5 ml (½ tsp) ground cumin
1–2 cloves garlic, crushed
5 ml (1 tsp) tomato puree
salt and black pepper
4 chicken portions, skinned

1. Place all the ingredients, except for the chicken in a bowl and mix thoroughly.

2. Place chicken portions in a dish and coat with the sauce. Cover, then marinade overnight.

3. Cook the chicken in a preheated oven at 220°C, LOW power microwave for 20–25 minutes, turning occasionally. Serve hot with salad.

——— COOK'S TIP ———
To allow more flavour to soak into the chicken, cut shallow slits in the flesh.

See photograph page 46

TURKEY AND PIMENTO STRUDEL

Needless to say, this recipe was developed one Christmas as yet another way of using up the never ending leftover turkey! It is ideal to serve at a New Year's Eve buffet party or even cold for lunch. The recipe is very versatile and can be adapted to suit your ingredients in the store cupboard. In the following recipe we have used uncooked turkey fillets which are readily available in supermarkets and mean you can also make this recipe at other times of the year.

Serves 4

225 g (8 oz) raw turkey fillet
125 g (4 oz) button mushrooms, sliced
1 × 190 g (6¾ oz) can pimentos, drained and sliced
30 ml (2 tbsp) double cream
2.5 ml (½ tsp) dried rosemary
salt and black pepper
225 g (8 oz) puff pastry
beaten egg or milk to glaze

1. Chop the turkey fillet into approximately 2.5 cm (1 in) pieces. Place in a bowl with the mushrooms, pimento, cream, rosemary and seasoning. Mix thoroughly.

2. Roll out the pastry on a floured surface to a large square approximately 35 cm (14 in).

3. Spoon the filling all over the pastry leaving approximately 2.5 cm (1 in) around the edges.

4. Brush the edges with beaten egg or milk, then fold 2.5 cm (1 in) at the sides and roll up from one end.

5. Place on a baking dish, brush with egg or milk and bake in a preheated oven at 200°C, LOW power microwave for 20 minutes.

TURKEY LEGS WITH CRANBERRY AND APPLE STUFFING

Turkey, as Bernard Matthews often reminds us, can be eaten the whole year round and is a very economical meat. Turkey legs can usually be bought from large supermarkets, but your local butcher may also have them, if you ask him. They are not often on display, but our butcher produced some immediately from 'round the back'. More often than not they seem to be frozen, and need to be thoroughly defrosted before you attempt to bone them.

Serves 4

4 turkey drumsticks
2 rashers, smoked streaky bacon, chopped
15 ml (1 level tbsp) celery, finely chopped
15 ml (1 level tbsp) onion, finely chopped
1 eating apple, peeled, cored and chopped
25 g (1 oz) breadcrumbs
30 ml (2 tbsp) cranberry sauce
salt and black pepper
butter

Sauce

10 ml (2 level tsp) plain flour
225 ml (8 fl oz) chicken or turkey stock
75 ml (2 fl oz) medium sherry

To garnish

1 eating apple, sliced
lemon juice

1. Cut the turkey drumsticks lengthways along the bone, and with a sharp knife remove the bone and as many 'tough' tendons as possible. Spread out on a chopping board, cover with cling film and beat with a rolling pin to flatten slightly.

2. Place the bacon, celery and onion in a dish and cook on HIGH power in the microwave for 2 minutes. Stir in the apple, breadcrumbs, cranberry sauce and seasoning.

3. Spread the stuffing over the boned drumsticks and roll up. Secure with cocktail sticks or tie into neat parcels with string.

4. Place in a shallow dish, dot with butter and cook in a preheated oven at 220°C, LOW power microwave for 20 minutes, or until clear juice runs from the meat when a skewer is inserted into it. Turn and baste the meat occasionally.

5. Remove the drumsticks from the oven and place on a warm serving dish. To make the sauce, strain 15 ml (1 tbsp) of the cooking juices from the dish into a bowl and stir in the flour. Blend in the stock and sherry and return to the oven on HIGH power for 3–4 minutes, whisking thoroughly when cooked.

6. Remove the cocktail sticks or string from the drumsticks, pour over the sauce and serve, garnished with slices of apple, dipped in lemon juice.

—— VARIATION ——
Use a favourite stuffing of your own choice to fill the drumsticks. A chestnut stuffing is always good.

BONED STUFFED TURKEY

Although it takes a little time to bone and stuff the turkey, it pays off a hundred fold on Christmas Day! The turkey is easy to carve and there are no bones to sort out afterwards. A friendly butcher may be persuaded to bone the turkey (do not ask him on Christmas Eve!) but as long as you have a good sharp knife and a little patience, it is very easy and extremely rewarding. The following are some ideas for stuffings – use 2 of the stuffings so that you have a colourful and flavoursome filling.

Serves 10

1×3.5 kg (8 lb) fresh turkey
seasonings
2 stuffings (see below)

1. Make 2 of the stuffings and set aside.

2. With a sharp knife slit down the centre of the underside. Cut the flesh from the carcass using short sharp strokes.

3. When the leg joint is reached cut through the ball and socket joint, leaving the leg bone with the meat.

4. Sever the wing joint from the carcass and leave that in.

5. Continue cutting until you get to the breast bone. Be careful not to cut the skin.

6. Repeat with the other side. Then place the carcass in the stock pot.

7. Now bone the leg cutting the flesh away until you can pull the bone through turning the leg inside out. Do the same with the wings and the other leg. You now have a flat piece of meat with legs and wings tucked in.

8. Remove the breast fillets and lay the stuffings on the meat. Place the fillets back onto the stuffing.

9. Roll the turkey up and sew together or tie with string.

10. Roast upside down at 180°C, LOW power microwave for 40 minutes, turn over and roast for another 30 minutes, 180°C, LOW power microwave. When pierced the juices should run clear.

11. Make gravy from the stock and roasting juices.

——— COOK'S TIP ———
Bone the fresh turkey well in advance and freeze unstuffed. Make a good bone stock and freeze that also discarding the bones. Make the stuffings the day before and keep cool. Stuff and roll the turkey just before cooking.

STUFFINGS

Mushroom and liver

125 g (4 oz) onion
2 cloves garlic
50 g (2 oz) butter
225 g (8 oz) chicken or turkey liver
125 g (6 oz) button mushrooms, chopped
30 ml (2 level tbsp) parsley, chopped
125 g (4 oz) fresh brown breadcrumbs
1 egg
salt and pepper

1. Chop the onion finely, crush the garlic and saute them in the butter, in a dish on HIGH power microwave for 3 minutes.

2. Chop the liver, add to the dish, with the chopped mushrooms, stir well and cook for a couple of minutes on HIGH power.

3. Add the parsley, breadcrumbs and the egg, season well and mix.

Cranberry sausage meat

50 g (2 oz) streaky bacon, chopped
1 small onion, chopped
175 g (6 oz) pork sausage meat
salt and pepper
45 ml (3 tbsp) cranberry and orange sauce
15 ml (1 level tbsp) parsley, chopped
75 g (3 oz) breadcrumbs
45 ml (3 tbsp) lemon juice

1. Fry the bacon in its own fat until crisp, 4 minutes on HIGH power. Remove from the pan, then fry the onion in the fat until soft, 3 minutes HIGH power.

2. Mix the bacon and onion with three remaining ingredients and use as a stuffing for turkey.

Rice and watercress

110 g (4 oz) long grain rice	
375 ml (¾ pt) turkey stock	
110 g (4 oz) streaky bacon, chopped	
1 bunch watercress, chopped	
50 g (2 oz) walnuts, chopped	
rind of 1 lemon	
salt and black pepper	
1 egg	

1. Cook the rice in the stock for 12–14 minutes on HIGH or until tender, then drain.

2. Fry the bacon in its own fat until crisp, 5 minutes HIGH power, then add with the fat to the rice along with all the remaining ingredients. Bind together with the egg and use as a stuffing.

Orange and raisin

1 small onion, chopped	
25 g (1 oz) butter	
grated rind of 1 orange	
50 g (2 oz) raisins	
30 ml (2 level tbsp) parsley, chopped	
2.5 ml (½ tsp) marjoram	
salt and pepper	
75 g (3 oz) breadcrumbs	
1 egg, beaten	

1. Fry the onion in the melted butter until soft, 3 minutes HIGH power then combine with the remaining ingredients. Use as a stuffing.

NORMANDY DUCK

Apples go very well with duck, as their sharpness is a good contrast to the richness of the meat. Use a very dry cider and, if available, a couple of tablespoons of Calvados really make it special.

Serves 4

1 2.25 kg (5 lb) duck	
1 large cooking apple	
450 ml (¾ pt) dry cider	
25 g (1 oz) butter	
25 g (1 oz) flour	
150 ml (¼ pt) single cream	
30 ml (2 tbsp) Calvados	

To garnish

red skinned apple slices, dipped in lemon juice

1. Prick the duck well, stuff with the chopped apple and place upside down on a trivet in a roasting dish. Cook in the preheated oven at 220°C, MEDIUM power for 30 minutes.

2. Remove the trivet. Drain the duck and turn over. Pour over the cider and cook at 220°C, MEDIUM power microwave for 25 minutes, basting occasionally.

3. Remove the duck when cooked and cut into 4 joints when cooled a little. Try to remove as many bones from the inside of the duck portions. Keep warm.

4. Strain the cider and the apples through a sieve and remove as much fat as possible.

5. Melt the butter in a casserole in the microwave on HIGH for 1½ minutes.

6. Stir in the flour, microwave on HIGH for 1 minute.

7. Stir in the cider and whisk until smooth. Microwave on HIGH for 3 minutes or until boiling, stirring after every minute.

8. Stir in the cream and Calvados if used, mix well, add the duck joints and warm gently for 3 minutes on HIGH power. Do not boil.

9. Serve accompanied by a plain vegetable and garnished with apple slices.

DUCK WITH ORANGE SAUCE

Duck can often be disappointing; there is not a lot of meat and it can often be rather tough. Not anymore! The combination oven browns and crisps and the microwaves break down the fat. The result is delicious, tender and quick. We have given instructions for making the sauce in the conventional manner; however if your microwave is free, use it to make the sauce. Duck with orange sauce is a perennial favourite and marmalade really improves it.

Serves 4

1 large orange
1 2.25 kg (5 lb) duck
15 ml (1 tbsp) runny honey
1 carrot
1 onion
1 bayleaf
150 ml (¼ pt) orange juice
25 g (1 oz) butter
25 g (1 oz) flour
30 ml (2 tbsp) marmalade
salt and pepper

To garnish

watercress
orange slices to serve

1. With a potato peeler, peel the orange and cut into fine julienne strips.

2. Cut the remaining pith off the orange and place the orange segments inside the breast cavity of the duck. Prick the duck well.

3. Put the duck upside down on a trivet in a roasting dish. Cook, in a hot oven at 220°C, MEDIUM power microwave for 30 minutes.

4. Drain the fat off and discard then turn the duck and cook for another 20 minutes at 220°C, MEDIUM power microwave. Ten minutes before the end spread the honey over the duck.

5. Meanwhile put the giblets, carrot, onion, bayleaf and seasoning into a saucepan with 600 ml (1 pt) water. Bring to the boil and simmer for 40 minutes.

6. When the duck is cooked, place it on a serving dish and tent with foil to keep it warm.

7. Separate the fat from the meat juices and discard. Make the orange juice and meat juices up to 600 ml (1 pt) with the giblet stock.

8. Melt the butter in a saucepan, add the flour and cook for 30 seconds. Remove from the heat and gradually add the liquid.

9. Return to the heat and bring to the boil stirring constantly. Add the julienne strips of peel and the marmalade. Season to taste and simmer gently for 2 minutes for the flavours to develop.

—— S E R V I N G   S U G G E S T I O N ——
Serve the duck garnished with watercress and orange slices and accompanied by the sauce. We prefer to serve creamed potatoes and plain vegetables with this because duck is rather rich.

See cover photograph

PHEASANT AND RED WINE GOUGERE

It is often difficult to estimate how many pheasant are needed to serve at a dinner party. If you get it wrong and there are left overs, this recipe can use them to feed four without losing the wonderful flavour of the bird.

Serves 4

25 g (1 oz) butter
1 small onion, finely chopped
125 g (4 oz) smoked back bacon
125 g (4 oz) button mushrooms, sliced
15 ml (1 level tbsp) plain flour
150 ml (¼ pt) stock
150 ml (¼ pt) red wine
225 g (8 oz) cooked pheasant, roughly chopped
salt and black pepper

Choux pastry

150 ml (¼ pt) water

50 g (2 oz) butter

65 g (2½ oz) plain flour

2 eggs, lightly beaten

50 g (2 oz) cheese, grated

1. Melt the butter in a shallow dish, suitable for serving the gougere in, on HIGH power for 1 minute.

2. Stir in the onion, bacon and mushrooms and cook for 4 minutes, stirring occasionally. Stir in the flour, then gradually blend in the stock and wine. Return to the microwave on HIGH power for 4–5 minutes, stirring halfway through the cooking time.

3. Stir in the pheasant, and season to taste. Set aside while making the choux pastry.

4. Place the water and butter in a bowl and heat on HIGH power for 4 minutes, or until the butter has melted and the water boiling. Shoot in the flour and beat until the mixture leaves the sides of the bowl.

5. Cool slightly, then gradually beat in the eggs, a little at a time. Beat in the cheese, then spoon or pipe around the pheasant mixture. Bake in a preheated oven at 200°C, LOW power microwave for 18 minutes. Serve immediately.

—— COOK'S TIP ——
The choux pastry can be made on the hot plate while the oven is preheating.

PIGEON WITH REDCURRANT SAUCE

Pigeon are a delicious game bird and so inexpensive that they really should make a regular appearance on the dinner table. They are more usually casseroled as they can be tough, but if young birds are chosen (with pink legs), they can be successfully roasted.

Serves 4

4 young pigeon, dressed

butter

Sauce

15 g (½ oz) butter

1 small onion, peeled and finely chopped

150 ml (¼ pt) chicken stock

150 ml (¼ pt) port

30 ml (2 tbsp) redcurrant jelly

15 ml (1 level tbsp) arrowroot

salt and black pepper

To serve

4 croutons approximately 1 cm (½ in) thick and similar in size to the pigeon

watercress

1. Wipe the birds, then put a good knob of butter inside each one.

2. Place in a roasting dish, breast side down, and dot thoroughly with more butter. Cook in a preheated oven at 190°C, LOW power microwave for approximately 30 minutes, depending on the size of the birds. Turn over after 20 minutes.

3. To make the sauce, melt the butter in a saucepan and gently saute the onion for 2–3 minutes. Add the stock, port and redcurrant jelly and bring to the boil, stirring to dissolve the jelly. Remove from the heat.

4. Blend the arrowroot with a little water and stir into the sauce. Return to the heat and stir until the sauce clears and thickens.

5. Serve the pigeon on croutons, accompanied by the sauce and garnished with watercress.

—— COOK'S TIP ——
The sauce can be made in advance and reheated at the last minute in the microwave.

See photograph page 47

ROAST PHEASANT WITH BACON

Pheasants are not native to Britain and these days in fact they are bred specially. During the winter when game is in season it is rather nice to eat pheasant occasionally. They are easy to cook and make a change. They are sold by the brace, that is a cock and a hen bird, and if they are to be roasted like this they should be hung quite well to improve the flavour. Pheasants are low in fat as is most game, so that these days when we are so conscious of the need to limit fat intake they become doubly attractive.

Serves 6–8

| 1 brace of pheasants |
| 10 rashers of streaky bacon |

1. Pluck and draw the pheasants and wipe out the insides.

2. Cover the breasts of the birds with bacon and place in a roasting dish. Roast in a preheated oven at 200°C, LOW power microwave for between 30–35 minutes (only once have we had a brace of birds that took as long as 40 minutes).

3. Serve the birds with a little clear gravy made from the roasting juices and giblet stock boiled to reduce.

GAME PIE

Raised pies always summon up images of a farmhouse kitchen we know up in Yorkshire, which was a hive of activity when the fattened pigs were killed. The hooks are still in the ceiling where the ham was hung to cure and apparently hours were spent raising pies using the traditional wooden pie moulds. You steadied the mould with your chin, leaving both hands free to raise up the pastry – consequently there were lots of blistered chins! The wooden moulds are still on display in the kitchen and are used on occasion. The game meat in the following recipe makes a rich pie, but do go back to the traditional pork pie as an alternative.

Serves 6–8

Pastry

| 350 g (12 oz) plain flour |
| salt |
| 1 egg yolk |
| 150 ml (¼ pt) milk and water mixed |
| 100 g (4 oz) lard |

Filling

| 275 g (10 oz) game meat, chopped (pheasant, partridge, pigeon etc.) |
| 175 g (6 oz) belly of pork, chopped |
| 2.5 ml (½ tsp) mixed herbs |
| salt and black pepper |
| 15 ml (1 tbsp) red wine |

To glaze

| 1 egg, beaten |

Jellied stock

| 70 ml (2½ fl oz) stock |
| 5 ml (1 level tsp) gelatine |

1. Mix together all the filling ingredients and leave to marinade for several hours or overnight.

2. To make the pastry, place the flour and salt in a mixing bowl and mix in the egg yolk.

3. Place the milk and lard in a bowl and heat on HIGH power for 3–4 minutes or until boiling. Pour over the flour and mix together.

4. As soon as the pastry is cool enough to handle, knead together lightly, then cut off a quarter and set aside for the lid.

5. Wrap a piece of grease-proof paper around a large jar (approximately 12.5 cm [5 in] in diameter). Flatten the pastry into a circle, stand on a greased tray then stand the jar in the centre and gently raise the pastry up the sides of the jar to a height of about 10 cm (4 in). Cool slightly, then remove the jar and paper.

6. Pack the meat into the pastry shell; if the pastry feels a little soft, wrap a piece of grease-proof paper around the outside and tie with string.

7. Brush the edges with the beaten egg then roll out the remaining pastry to form a lid, reserving any trimmings for leaves. Put the lid on top of the pie, sealing the edges with a fork.

8. Cut a small hole in the centre of the pie to allow steam to escape, then brush with the egg and decorate with pastry leaves. Bake at 180°C, LOW power microwave for 40 minutes, removing the grease-proof paper halfway through and brushing the sides with egg.

9. When the pie has cooled, make the jellied stock by softening the gelatine in the stock on HIGH power for 30 seconds. Allow to stand for 5 minutes, and if the gelatine has not softened sufficiently repeat the process. Allow the stock to cool until just beginning to set, then pour through the hole in the centre of the pie.

VARIATION

Use similar quantities of veal and ham with a pinch of mixed herbs to fill the pie.

RABBIT TAGINE WITH PRUNES

Rabbit is very underused, yet it is very lean, so ideal if you are trying to cut down your fat intake. It is delicious and serving it with prunes and carrots makes it also look delicious. This recipe is based on a Moroccan dish, Tagine being the name of the casserole they use.

Serves 4

30 ml (2 tbsp) olive oil
1 medium onion, sliced
2 cloves of garlic, sliced
5 ml (1 level tsp) cinnamon
5 ml (1 level tsp) ginger
10 ml (2 level tsp) cumin
1 rabbit cut into small pieces or 450 g (1 lb) rabbit, boned
225 g (8 oz) carrots, cut in 1.2 cm (½ in) pieces
225 g (8 oz) prunes
the rind of ½ lemon (use a potato peeler)
450 ml (15 fl oz) chicken stock
salt and pepper

1. Place the olive oil, onion and garlic in a large casserole and microwave on HIGH for 3–4 minutes until the onion has started to soften.

2. Stir in the spices and cook for 1 minute on HIGH.

3. Put all the other ingredients into the casserole and cover with a lid, cook at 170°C, HIGH power microwave for 5 minutes then 170°C, LOW power microwave for 45 minutes.

4. Serve with rice or couscous.

Vegetables and Vegetarian Meals

Vegetables are so versatile they no longer have to be just an accompaniment to a meal. With the addition of extra ingredients they can become highly nutritious meals in their own right. You do not have to be a vegetarian to enjoy the refreshing change that vegetable meals bring to your diet. Your pocket will also appreciate the low cost of many of the interesting recipes in this section which come from many parts of the world.

Fresh vegetables are generally best cooked on microwave alone which preserves their natural flavour and colour, and because of the small amount of cooking liquid required there is less loss of nutrients.

Cooking times for fresh vegetables, using the microwave only, can be found in the vegetable cooking chart.

When planning vegetarian meals, however, a contrast in textures can be important, and the combination oven enables you to do this. It is easy to achieve a crisp topping without over cooking the vegetables.

Left to right: Zyldyk casserole (page 76); Vegetable lasagne (page 80); Wholemeal cheese crown (page 91).

64

POMMES ANNA

What a wonderful and simple way of serving the good old potato! One would think that although some vegetables are not always readily available in our local green grocers, there is never a problem buying potatoes. This is true, but which potato of the several different varieties do we choose? It depends very much on the recipe – what is good for mashing is not necessarily good for chips. The following recipe calls for 'waxy' potatoes which will hold together well to form the potato cake. A good variety to use are Desiree or 'reds'.

Serves 6

900 g (2 lb) potatoes

50 g (2 oz) butter

salt and freshly ground black pepper·

To serve

chopped parsley

1. Peel the potatoes and slice thinly preferably using a food processor or mandolin slicer.

2. Melt the butter on HIGH power in the microwave for 1–1½ minutes.

3. Line the base of a 20 cm (8 in) cake tin or oven-proof dish with grease-proof paper, then brush thoroughly with melted butter.

4. Place a layer of potatoes in the tin, then brush with butter and season with salt and pepper. Repeat until all the potato is used up. Cover with a buttered circle of grease-proof paper.

5. Cook in a preheated oven at 220°C, LOW power microwave for 30 minutes, removing the grease-proof paper halfway through the cooking time.

Courgette kayaks (page 71); Steak and kidney pie (page 36); Heart with peppers (page 51).

PREVIOUS PAGE
Beouf en croute (page 34); Sate pork accompanied by chilli sauce (page 41) and Spare ribs (page 43) with rice; Lamb in burgundy (page 38).

6. Turn out the potato cake onto a serving plate, crisp side upper most and sprinkle with chopped parsley. Serve cut into wedges.

———— COOK'S TIP ————

For roast potatoes around the meat; peel potatoes and cut into even sized pieces then toss in a little oil and add to the roasting pan 30 minutes before the meat is cooked. Cook on combination using a LOW power and fairly hot temperature. Turn the potatoes occasionally.

See photograph page 28

POMMES LYONNAISE

A useful potato dish for the end of the season when the potatoes are large, it is quick and easy to do particularly if you have a food processor, mandolin or even a cheese grater with a slicing side to it.

This dish can be varied with the addition of cheese on top or in the layers to turn it into a tasty supper dish.

Serves 4

25 g (1 oz) butter

650 g (1½ lb) potatoes

1 clove of garlic, crushed

small onion, finely sliced

salt & pepper

200 ml (⅓ pt) milk or cream

1. Melt the butter in a 20 cm (8 in) oven-proof dish on HIGH power for 1 minute, brush it round the dish.

2. Slice the potatoes thinly and layer with the garlic, onion and seasonings in the dish finishing with a potato layer.

3. Pour on the milk or cream.

4. Bake in a preheated oven 180°C HIGH power microwave for 16–20 minutes or until the potatoes are tender and the top golden.

5. Garnish with parsley.

See photograph page 47

COMBINATION ROSTI

This is a quick way of cooking potatoes to make a nice change. It is based on the Swiss potato dish but cooked in the oven instead. For a bit of variation add a layer of cheese in the middle.

Serves 4–6

25 g (1 oz) butter, melted

900 g (2 lb) potatoes, peeled

salt and pepper

1. Brush a 20 cm (8 in) dish with the butter and pack in the potatoes, grated, seasoning between layers.

2. Sprinkle the remaining butter over the top.

3. Bake in a preheated oven at 200°C, LOW power microwave for 25 minutes.

HARLEQUIN PARSNIPS

The humble parsnip is often neglected, which is a great shame as it is such an economical winter vegetable, full of goodness and extremely versatile. It is delicious roasted around a joint, pureed, or served as fritters. The following recipe can be served as an accompaniment to roast meats or as a meal in itself.

Serves 6

30 ml (2 tbsp) oil

675 g (1½ lb) parsnips, peeled and sliced

butter

30 ml (2 level tbsp) soft brown sugar

salt and black pepper

150 ml (¼ pt) single cream

450 g (1 lb) tomatoes, skinned and sliced

125 g (4 oz) cheese, grated

50 g (2 oz) fresh brown breadcrumbs

1. Heat the oil in a large saucepan and gently fry the parsnips for a few minutes.

2. Butter a 1.8 lit (3 pt) casserole dish then place a layer of parsnips in the base.

3. Sprinkle the parsnips with a little sugar, salt, pepper and cream. Cover with a layer of tomatoes and then cheese. Repeat these layers, ending with cheese.

4. Sprinkle over the breadcrumbs, dot generously with butter and cook in a preheated oven at 180°C, LOW power microwave for 30 minutes. Serve immediately.

— SERVING SUGGESTION —
For roast parsnips around the meat; peel the parsnips and cut into sticks, toss in oil then add to the meat pan 15–20 minutes before the meat is cooked. Cook on combination using a LOW power level and a fairly high temperature.

FENNEL IN RED LENTIL PUREE

A book recently described fennel as a 'common vegetable', which is extremely unjust! It is neither 'common' as far as availability goes, although this is certainly improving and most big supermarkets now stock it, nor common in flavour.
Its unusual, slightly aniseed flavour goes extremely well with fish dishes, but it can also be served with light meats. It is delicious simply boiled, or served with a white sauce, but the following recipe makes a substantial and unusual vegetarian dish.

Serves 4

2 bulbs of fennel, approximately 450 g (1 lb) in weight
25 g (1 oz) butter
1 onion, peeled and chopped
175 g (6 oz) red lentils
salt and freshly ground black pepper
25 g (1 oz) fresh breadcrumbs
25 g (1 oz) cheese, grated

1. Trim the fennel then cut into chunks, about 3.8 cm (1½ in) in size. Place in a casserole dish with 30 ml (2 tbsp) water and cook on HIGH power for 4 minutes. Set aside.

2. Melt the butter in a casserole dish on HIGH power for 1 minute, then add the onion and return to the microwave on HIGH power for 2 minutes.

3. Rinse the lentils, then add to the onion with 450 ml (¾ pt) water. Cook on HIGH power for 8 minutes.

4. Pour the lentils into a liquidizer and add the liquid from the fennel. Puree until smooth, adding salt and pepper to taste.

5. Pour the puree over the fennel, mix together the breadcrumbs and cheese and sprinkle over the top. Bake in a preheated oven at 200°C, MEDIUM power microwave for 15 minutes.

COURGETTE KAYAKS

These colourful vegetables make a tasty and attractive vegetable dish to go with a meat or fish course. Alternatively, with the addition of cheese they can be served as a vegetarian or supper dish. They are quick and easy to prepare and because of the speed of cooking, all the colours are brightened.

Serves 4

4 medium sized courgettes (approx 450 g [1 lb] in weight)
50 g (2 oz) butter
1 clove garlic, crushed
1 small onion, finely chopped
50 g (2 oz) wholemeal breadcrumbs
2 large tomatoes, chopped
2.5 ml (½ level tsp) basil
15 ml (1 level tbsp) parsley, chopped
salt and black pepper

1. Wash the courgettes and top and tail them, then cut in half lengthways, and scoop out the inside with a spoon.

2. Place the courgettes in a shallow dish and chop the flesh.

3. Melt the butter on HIGH power in a mixing bowl, then stir in the garlic, onion and courgette flesh. Cook on HIGH power for 2 minutes.

4. Stir in the remaining ingredients, then use to fill the courgette shells. Cook in a preheated oven at 220°C, MEDIUM power microwave for 8 minutes, or until the courgettes are tender.

───── COOK'S TIP ─────
Sprinkle over 50 g (2 oz) of grated cheese before going into the oven for a more substantial supper dish. For non vegetarians, a little chopped smoked bacon added with the onions at the beginning of the recipe is a nice addition.
For those ovens with a grill this recipe can be cooked using grill and microwave only.

See photograph page 68

RUSSIAN CABBAGE PIE

Do not let the cabbage conjure up visions of institutional vegetables, this is altogether different and very good. It looks rather nice and is certainly unusual. It is also quite cheap to make.

Serves 6

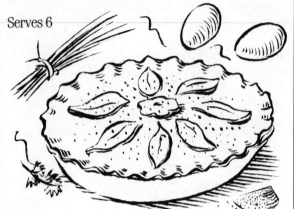

Pastry

225 g (8 oz) light wholemeal self raising flour

5 ml (1 level tsp) salt

50 g (2 oz) lard

50 g (2 oz) margarine

60 ml (4 tbsp) water to bind

Filling

50 g (2 oz) butter

1 medium onion, finely chopped

450 g (1 lb) cabbage, finely shredded

125 g (4 oz) mushrooms, sliced

5 ml (1 level tsp) chives

2 hard boiled eggs, shelled and chopped

5 ml (1 level tsp) sugar

salt and pepper

15 ml (1 level tbsp) parsley, chopped

egg for brushing

poppy seeds

1. Rub the fat into the flour. Add the water to make a pastry. Chill for 10 minutes.

2. Roll ⅔ of the pastry out to line a 20 cm (8 in) pie dish. Roll out the other ⅓ to make a lid; set aside.

3. Melt the butter in a large bowl, HIGH power for 1 minute, add the onion and cook on HIGH power for 3 minutes, stirring once.

4. Add the cabbage to the onion, cover and microwave on HIGH for 3 minutes.

5. Add the mushrooms and microwave on HIGH power for 2 minutes. The vegetables should be just tender.

6. Add the chives, eggs, sugar, seasoning and parsley, mixing well.

7. Cool and put the filling into the pastry case. Damp the edges and put the lid on. Brush with egg and sprinkle with poppy seeds.

8. Bake at 200°C, LOW power microwave for 16–20 minutes.

SERVING SUGGESTION
Serve hot or warm with soured cream or tomato sauce.

STUFFED CABBAGE LEAVES

A variation on the popular Mediterranean stuffed vine leaves. Cabbage leaves are a good substitute and because of their size, the filling can be more substantial. The meat can be stretched by the addition of breadcrumbs.

Serves 4

1 aubergine

salt and pepper

8 green cabbage leaves

15 ml (1 tbsp) oil

1 onion, peeled and chopped

350 g (12 oz) minced lamb

30 ml (2 tbsp) tomato puree

2.5 ml (½ tsp) coriander

8 slices Edam cheese, approximately 7.5 cm (3 in) square

Sauce

1 × 400 g (14 oz) can tomatoes

15 ml (1 level tbsp) parsley, chopped

1. Peel and slice the aubergine, sprinkle with salt and leave to stand for ½ hour. Rinse in cold water then drain thoroughly on kitchen paper. Chop.

2. Rinse the cabbage leaves then place in a shallow dish, cover and cook on HIGH power for 3 minutes.

3. Place the oil in a casserole dish and stir in the onion, aubergine and mince. Cover and cook on HIGH power for 4 minutes, stirring occasionally.

4. Drain any extra fat, then stir in the tomato puree and coriander. Season to taste.

5. Place a slice of cheese on each cabbage leaf, then top with the meat mixture. Fold each leaf into a parcel and place in a shallow dish.

6. Pour the tomatoes into a liquidizer and blend until smooth. Add the parsley and season. Pour over the cabbage parcels, then bake in a preheated oven at 180°C, MEDIUM power microwave for 15 minutes.

VARIATION

For a vegetarian dish, use a mixture of soaked bulgar wheat and vegetables to fill the cabbage leaves.

See photograph page 25

WHOLE CABBAGE STUFFED WITH RICE AND PINE KERNELS

In France stuffed cabbage is a very popular dish, usually stuffed with meat. This vegetarian version uses pine kernels and brown rice instead. Pine kernels are expensive to buy but delicious; only buy as many as you need at a time or keep them in the freezer.

Serves 6

1 green cabbage, 650 g (1½ lb)
75 g (3 oz) brown rice, cooked
1 onion, chopped finely
50 g (2 oz) butter
50 g (2 oz) pine kernels
1 egg
salt and pepper
300 ml (½ pt) vegetable stock
2 carrots, sliced
2 sticks celery, sliced

1. Trim the cabbage and cut out the hard stalk. Boil a large saucepan full of water and plunge the whole cabbage in. Boil again for 5 minutes.

2. Drain the cabbage and hollow out the centre leaving the outside leaves. Chop up the cabbage you remove.

3. Put the chopped onion and butter together in a mixing bowl and microwave on HIGH for 3 minutes. Mix in the chopped cabbage, pine kernels, salt, pepper and egg.

4. Fill the hollowed out cabbage with the stuffing and tie up with string.

5. Place the cabbage in a casserole with the carrots, celery and stock. Cover it with a lid.

6. Bake at 180°C, MEDIUM power microwave for 30 minutes or until the cabbage is tender. Serve cut into wedges with some of the casserole juices.

CARROT AND SWEDE RING WITH PARSLEY SAUCE

This way of serving carrot and swede turns them into a gourmet-style dish. The ring looks really attractive on the dinner table and tastes delicious. Because the vegetables are so interestingly presented a very simple meat or fish dish can accompany them, or with the addition of cheese, a vegetarian can be served.

Serves 4

225 g (½ lb) swede, peeled and chopped into small cubes

225 g (½ lb) carrots, peeled and thinly sliced

30 ml (2 tbsp) water

2 eggs, separated

40 g (1½ oz) butter

25 g (1 oz) flour

60 ml (4 tbsp) milk

salt and black pepper

Sauce

25 g (1 oz) butter

25 g (1 oz) flour

300 ml (½ pt) milk

15 ml (1 level tbsp) parsley, chopped

1. Place the swede and carrots in a casserole dish with the water, cover and cook on HIGH power for 6 minutes or until tender.

2. Drain, then puree in a liquidizer or food processor along with the egg yolks.

3. Place the 40 g (1½ oz) of butter in a bowl and melt on HIGH for 1 minute. Stir in the flour then blend in the milk. Cook on HIGH for 1½ minutes, then beat thoroughly. Beat into the swede and carrot mixture and season to taste.

4. Whisk the egg white until stiff, then fold into the swede and carrot mixture. Pour into a buttered 17.5–20 cm (7–8 in) ring mould and cook in a preheated oven at 200°C, LOW power microwave for 12 minutes.

5. While the ring is cooking, make the sauce on the hob. Melt the butter in a saucepan, then stir in the flour and cook for a minute. Gradually blend in the milk, stirring continuously. Bring to the boil and stir until thickened and smooth. Add the parsley and season to taste.

6. Turn out the ring and serve coated with parsley sauce.

--- **VARIATION** ---

Beat some grated cheese into the swede and carrot mixture or into sauce. Arrange blanched slices of courgette in the base of the ring mould before adding the swede and carrot mixture.

CELERY AND BROCCOLI PIE WITH TOMATO SAUCE

This pie has a rich cheesy pastry and a tasty vegetable filling. It is unusual and colourful. Serve it on a pool of the tomato sauce; it will not need anything else.

Serves 6

Tomato sauce

1 small onion, grated

1×400 g (14 oz) tin tomatoes

salt and pepper

pinch of mixed herbs

150 ml (5 fl oz) water

Filling

4 sticks of celery

225 g (8 oz) broccoli

50 g (2 oz) cheese, grated

30 ml (2 tbsp) of the tomato sauce

salt and pepper

Pastry

225 g (8 oz) plain flour	
50 g (2 oz) margarine	
50 g (2 oz) lard	
75 g (3 oz) cheese, grated	
2.5 ml (½ tsp) mustard	
60 ml (4 tbsp) water	

1. Put all the sauce ingredients in a casserole and microwave on HIGH for 10 minutes then MEDIUM for 10 minutes, cool slightly, then liquidize and if desired push through a sieve for a really smooth sauce.

2. Slice the celery and put it in a bowl with 30 ml (2 tbsp) of water, microwave on HIGH for 3 minutes, then add the thinly sliced broccoli stalks and florets. Microwave on HIGH for 3 minutes.

3. Drain and stir in the cheese, seasoning and the 30 ml (2 tbsp) of the tomato sauce.

4. Rub the fat into the flour until like breadcrumbs, stir in the cheese and mustard and then the water.

5. Knead the pastry lightly and roll ⅔ out to line a 20 cm (8 in) pie dish.

6. Put the filling into the lined pie dish and cover with the remaining ⅓ of pastry rolled out for a lid. Damp the edges so they stick and decorate with the trimmings. Brush with milk.

7. Bake in a preheated oven at 180°C, LOW power microwave for 18–25 minutes or until golden. Serve warm.

IMAN BAYILDI
(The Iman fainted)

This is a Turkish dish which should be eaten warm or cold. Ideally, if you can resist, leave it until the next day for the flavours to develop.
The rather curious name comes from a legend which

says that a holy man smelt this dish and was so overcome with the fragrance that he fainted; not very believable but a nice story.

Serves 6

3 medium sized long aubergines, approx 675 g (1½ lb) in weight	
salt	
3 medium onions, thinly sliced	
2×400 g (14 oz) tins tomatoes, drained	
3 fat garlic cloves	
90 ml (6 tbsp) olive oil	

1. With a potato peeler cut 3 or 4 strips of peel longways from the aubergines.

2. Cut the aubergines in half lengthways and cut across the cut side 3 or 4 times at 2.5 cm (1 in) intervals.

3. Place the aubergines in a bowl, sprinkle generously with salt and cover with cold water and a plate to keep them down. Leave for at least ½ hour.

4. Put the finely sliced onions separated into rings, into a bowl and sprinkle generously with salt. Leave for ½ hour.

5. Drain the aubergines and dry.

6. Rinse the onions and dry. Then mix with the tomatoes and chopped garlic.

7. Put 30 ml (2 tbsp) olive oil in the base of the oven proof dish large enough to take the aubergines in a single layer.

8. Put in the aubergines and pile on the onion mixture. Sprinkle with the remaining oil.

9. Bake at 170°C, HIGH power microwave for 10 minutes then 170°C, MEDIUM power for 30 minutes or until tender. Leave to cool in the dish and serve from it.

—— **VARIATION** ——
Five minutes before the end uncover and lay on some sliced mozzarella cheese, then finish the cooking time.

ZYLDYK CASSEROLE

Holland is renowned for its cheese, but also for its wide variety of fresh vegetables, many grown out of season in the acres of greenhouses so a Dutch name for this colourful, substantial casserole makes sense.

Serves 4

1 onion, peeled and sliced

175 g (6 oz) carrots, peeled and sliced

175 g (6 oz) courgettes, sliced

175 g (6 oz) cauliflower, broken into florets

175 g (6 oz) white cabbage, shredded

Sauce

25 g (1 oz) butter

25 g (1 oz) plain flour

milk

175 g (6 oz) Edam cheese, grated

10 ml (2 level tsp) curry powder

salt and black pepper

Topping

225 g (8 oz) frozen spinach, defrosted and drained

50 g (2 oz) fresh breadcrumbs

1. Place all the vegetables in a 1.8 lit (3 pt) casserole dish and pour over 150 ml (¼ pt) boiling water. Cover and cook on HIGH power for 6 minutes, stirring occasionally. Drain, reserving the liquid.

2. Melt the butter in a bowl on HIGH power for 1 minute. Stir in the flour. Make up the vegetable cooking liquid to 300 ml (½ pt) with milk and blend into the butter and flour.

3. Return the sauce to the microwave on HIGH power for 4 minutes, stirring halfway through the cooking time, and again on completion. Stir in 100 g (4 oz) of the cheese and the curry powder. Season with black pepper then pour over the vegetables.

4. Season the spinach, then spread over the vegetables. Mix the breadcrumbs with the remaining cheese and spoon over the top. Bake in a preheated oven at 200°C, LOW power microwave for 15–20 minutes or until golden brown.

See photograph page 65

SPINACH AND POTATO WEDGE

This uses a potato pastry, which makes an interesting change. It has been very popular on our vegetarian courses at the cookery school, so if serving it to a vegetarian, make sure you use vegetarian cheese made with a non animal rennet. The pastry is inclined to toughen if cooked too long so serve it as soon as it is browned.

Serves 4

450 g (1 lb) potatoes

50 g (2 oz) onion

30 ml (2 tbsp) oil

275 g (10 oz) frozen spinach, defrosted

100 g (4 oz) cottage cheese

75 g (3 oz) fresh parmesan cheese, grated

2 eggs

salt and pepper

pinch of nutmeg

125 g (4 oz) self raising flour

2.5 ml (½ tsp) baking powder

1. Scrub the potatoes, prick and microwave ¾ of them on HIGH ¾ for 9 minutes or until soft. Peel and sieve them and leave to cool.

2. Peel and coarsely grate the remaining potato, add it to the onion and oil in a dish and microwave on HIGH for 3 minutes.

3. Drain the defrosted spinach well and add it to the onion mixture. Microwave on HIGH for 3 minutes.

4. Stir in the cottage cheese, 50 g (2 oz) of the parmesan, 1 egg, salt, pepper and nutmeg. Leave aside.

5. Add the flour and baking powder to the sieved potato, season and bind with the other egg. Knead gently to make a soft dough.

6. On a well floured board roll the pastry out to a 30 cm (12 in) square and trim the edges.

7. Pile the spinach mixture in the centre and bring the corners of the pastry to the centre, gently pressing the edges together.

8. Roll out the trimmings and decorate the parcel; sprinkle with the remaining cheese.

9. Put on a greased baking dish and cook in a preheated oven at 200°C, LOW power microwave for 20 minutes. Serve hot.

―――― COOK'S TIP ――――
You may find it easier to put the pastry on the baking dish before filling because it is rather soft.

CAULIFLOWER AND EGGS IN CAPER SAUCE

This is really a glorified cauliflower cheese, but the eggs and the caper sauce means it is more substantial and flavoursome. It makes a delicious supper dish to serve when cauliflowers are plentiful. If not, brussel sprouts can be used instead.

Serves 4

| 1 cauliflower, cut into florets |
| 2 hard boiled eggs |
| 40 g (1½ oz) butter |
| 40 g (1½ oz) flour |
| 450 ml (¾ pt) milk |
| 30 ml (2 level tbsp) capers, chopped |
| salt and black pepper |
| 50 g (2 oz) cheese, grated |
| 25 g (1 oz) fresh breadcrumbs |

1. Place the cauliflower in a casserole dish with 30 ml (2 tbsp) water. Cover and cook on HIGH power for 4 minutes. Drain.

2. Shell the hard boiled eggs, then quarter them and add to the casserole dish with the cauliflower.

3. Melt the butter in a bowl on HIGH power for 1 minute then stir in the flour and gradually blend in the milk. Cook on HIGH power for 5 minutes whisking thoroughly halfway through the cooking time and again on completion.

4. Stir the capers into the sauce, then season and pour over the cauliflower.

5. Mix together the cheese and breadcrumbs, then sprinkle over the cauliflower. Cook in a preheated

oven at 200°C, LOW power microwave for 15 minutes.

EGGS FLORENTINE

This is a nutritious dish ideal for supper or lunch or even as a starter. It just needs crusty bread to go with it. Do not cook the spinach in advance just defrost it and drain it well. That way it tastes really fresh. Spinach with nutmeg in it really makes a difference, so do try it.

Serves 2 as main course
Serves 4 as starter

| 275 g (10 oz) packet frozen spinach |
| salt and pepper |
| 1½ g (¼ tsp) nutmeg |
| 4 eggs |
| 25 g (1 oz) butter |
| 35 g (1½ oz) flour |
| 300 ml (½ pt) milk |
| 100 g (4 oz) cottage cheese |
| 50 g (2 oz) cheddar |
| 1 egg |
| salt and pepper |
| 25 g (1 oz) breadcrumbs |

1. Defrost the spinach well and drain it. Place it in the bottom of a 20 cm (8 in) dish, season and sprinkle with nutmeg.

2. Make 4 hollows and crack an egg into each.

3. Put the butter, flour and milk into a jug, mix and microwave on HIGH for 2 minutes. Whisk then microwave on HIGH for a further 3 minutes.

4. Add the seasoning and cottage cheese and pour into a liquidizer. Liquidize until smooth. Add the cheddar and the extra egg.

5. Pour the sauce over the eggs and spinach and sprinkle with breadcrumbs.

6. Cook in a preheated oven at 200°C, LOW power microwave for 16–20 minutes.

PARMIGIANA

This is a delicious and substantial Italian vegetable dish. We have experimented with this recipe without frying the aubergines, but they remain a little tough, so we think that it is worth the extra trouble.

Serves 4

900 g (2 lb) aubergines
salt and freshly ground black pepper
vegetable or olive oil
1 onion, peeled and finely chopped
2 sticks celery, finely chopped
225 g (8 oz) carrots, peeled and grated
1×400 g (14 oz) can tomatoes
10 ml (2 tsp) tomato puree
150 ml (¼ pt) white wine
2.5 ml (½ tsp) oregano
225 g (8 oz) mozzarella cheese, thinly sliced
75 g (3 oz) parmesan cheese, grated

1. Peel and slice the aubergines, then sprinkle with salt and leave to stand for ½ hour.

2. Meanwhile, place 15 ml (1 tbsp) of oil in a casserole dish and stir in the onion, celery and carrot. Cook on HIGH power for 4 minutes, stirring halfway through the cooking time.

3. Add the tomatoes, puree, wine, oregano and season to taste, then cook on HIGH power for 12 minutes, stirring occasionally.

4. Rinse the aubergines in cold water and dry thoroughly on kitchen paper, then heat some oil in a frying pan and quickly fry the aubergines on each side. Drain on kitchen paper.

5. Lightly grease a casserole dish then place a layer of aubergines in the base, cover with tomato sauce, then a layer of mozzarella. Sprinkle over a little

parmesan. Repeat the layers, sprinkling the remaining parmesan over the top then bake in a preheated oven at 200°C, LOW power microwave for 20 minutes.

ONIONS STUFFED WITH RAISINS AND OREGANO

Stuffed onion usually takes ages to cook, however with the combination oven they do not need part boiling first and with a grapefruit knife hollowing out is easy. The raisins add a little sweetness to the onions. Oregano goes very well with this, use fresh if available, but double the quantity, otherwise dried will do. Excellent with roast pork or roast lamb.

Serves 4

4 onions each about 175 g (6 oz)
50 g (2 oz) butter
50 g (2 oz) breadcrumbs
50 g (2 oz) cheese
25 g (1 oz) raisins
2.5 ml (½ tsp) oregano
salt and pepper

1. Peel the onions and using a grapefruit knife hollow out the centres. Chop up 2 of the centres.

2. Put the chopped onions with the butter and microwave on HIGH for 4 minutes.

3. Add all the other stuffing ingredients, mix well and divide between the 4 onions.

4. Put in a dish just big enough to hold them, add 30 ml (2 tbsp) water and cover with a lid.

5. Cook at 200°C, LOW power microwave for 25–30 minutes or until tender.

—— COOK'S TIP ——
Be careful when hollowing out the onions – too much and they will collapse – and leave the root intact to keep them together.

See photograph page 48

CHEESE AND CHIVE FLAN

This has an unusual crumbly pastry base, so do not worry if you cannot roll it out as pressing it out will do. It is much lighter than a normal wholemeal pastry and appeals to people who do not usually like 'ethnic' foods. Try the pastry base with other fillings.

Serves 6

Pastry

125 g (4 oz) medium oatmeal

125 g (4 oz) wholemeal flour

pinch of salt

125 g (4 oz) margarine

30–45 ml (2–3 tbsp) water

Filling

1 onion, finely sliced

15 ml (1 tbsp) oil

2 eggs

150 ml (¼ pt) milk

250 g (8 oz) cheddar cheese, grated

salt and pepper

15 ml (1 level tbsp) fresh chives or 5 ml (1 level tsp) dried

1. Rub the margarine into the oatmeal and flour until it resembles breadcrumbs.

2. Add the salt and water and mix to a firm dough.

3. Turn out onto a floured surface and knead until smooth. Roll out and line a 20 cm (8 in) flan tin. Chill whilst making the filling.

4. Saute the onion with the oil until soft (3 minutes on HIGH power microwave).

5. Spread the onions on the base of the flan. Top with the grated cheese and chives, chopped.

6. Mix together the eggs, milk, salt and pepper and pour over the flan.

7. Cook in a combination oven preheated to 200°C, LOW power microwave for 16–20 minutes until golden brown.

SPINACH AND CHEESE PIE

This is a variation on a traditional Greek recipe. It is absolutely delicious and very quick, in a combination oven. It uses filo pastry which can be bought frozen from a good delicatessen. You can make your own but it is impossible to get it as thin. Once you have tried this pastry you will start using it for other things.

Serves 6–8

45 ml (3 tbsp) olive oil

2 medium onions, finely chopped

350 g (12 oz) frozen spinach, defrosted

45 ml (3 level tbsp) parsley, chopped, (preferably Greek)

5 ml (1 level tsp) dried dill weed

2.5 ml (½ tsp) salt

freshly ground black pepper

50 g (2 oz) parmesan cheese, grated

175 g (6 oz) cheddar cut into small cubes

4 eggs, beaten

60 ml (4 tbsp) milk

125 g (¼ lb) soft margarine or butter, melted

16 sheets (about half a packet) filo pastry

1. Put the onions with the oil and microwave on HIGH for 3 minutes.

2. Stir in the defrosted spinach, the herbs, seasoning, eggs, milk and cheese.

3. Brush a dish with the melted margarine and layer in 8 pieces of filo, brushing each with the melted margarine or butter. Pour on the filling.

4. Repeat the remaining 8 pieces of filo, brushing the top well.

5. Bake in a preheated oven 190°C, LOW power microwave for 20 minutes. Serve hot and cut into squares.

RED LENTIL AND COURGETTE LOAF

Vegetarians and non-vegetarians alike will thoroughly enjoy this colourful and tasty loaf. It is simple to prepare and remains beautifully moist when cooked in the combination oven. Layer vegetables of your own choice between the lentil mixture, if preferred.

Serves 4–6

175 g (6 oz) red lentils
450 ml (¾ pt) water
1 onion, finely chopped
100 g (4 oz) cheese, grated
1 egg, lightly beaten
45 ml (3 tbsp) top of the milk
15 ml (1 level tbsp) parsley, chopped
2.5 ml (½ tsp) cayenne pepper
salt and black pepper
2 small courgettes

1. Rinse the lentils then place in a deep dish and cover with the water. Cook on HIGH for 12 minutes or until tender.

2. Beat all the remaining ingredients except for the courgettes into the lentils and season to taste.

3. Slice the courgettes thinly and place in a dish with 15 ml (1 tbsp) water. Cover and cook on HIGH for 3 minutes. Drain.

4. Grease a 450 g (1 lb) loaf dish or similar quantity small casserole dish, then spoon on ⅓ of the lentil mixture. Cover with half the courgettes then another ⅓ of the lentil mixture. Repeat with the remaining ingredients.

5. Bake in a preheated oven at 200°C, LOW power microwave for 30 minutes or until golden brown. Leave for a few minutes in the dish before turning out and serving.

VEGETABLE LASAGNE

Pasta cooks very well in the microwave and although cooking times may be no faster than conventionally, it does have the advantage of not filling the kitchen with steam! Seasonal vegetables of your own choice can be used for this recipe – our green grocer had stew packs on special offer, so these were the vegetables we chose!

Serves 4

175 g (6 oz) lasagne
salt and pepper
1 onion, sliced
225 g (8 oz) carrots, peeled and thinly sliced
2 small turnips, peeled and chopped
2 leeks, cleaned, trimmed and sliced
1 parsnip, peeled and thinly sliced

Sauce

50 g (2 oz) butter
50 g (2 oz) flour
600 ml (1 pt) milk
175 g (6 oz) cheese, grated

1. Cover the lasagne with boiling salted water and cook on HIGH power in the microwave for 8 minutes. Drain, rinse with cold water, spread out and set aside.

2. Place all the vegetables in a casserole dish, pour over 45 ml (3 tbsp) water and cook on HIGH power for 5 minutes, stirring halfway through the cooking time. Leave to stand.

3. To make the sauce, melt the butter in a bowl on HIGH power for 1½ minutes. Stir in the flour, then blend in the milk. Return to the oven on HIGH power for 6 minutes, whisking thoroughly halfway through the cooking time and again on completion. Stir 100 g (4 oz) of cheese into the sauce and season to taste.

4. Butter a dish approximately 25 cm (9 in) square, then layer alternately, cheese sauce, vegetables and lasagne. End with cheese sauce, then sprinkle over the remaining cheese. Bake in a preheated oven at 200°C, MEDIUM power microwave for 20 minutes.

See photograph page 65

Breads and Buns

Bread and yeast mixtures cooked in a combination oven are very successful. Not only is the cooking quicker, but the result is actually better than bread conventionally cooked.

Normally homemade bread has a wonderful flavour but is rather heavy. Shop bread is light but does not have the flavour of homemade bread. Using the combination oven you will find the bread light and tasty – be sure to make plenty, it goes rather fast.

Types of Yeast

Fresh yeast – This is easy to use but it is becoming difficult to find, although your local baker may stock it. It gives the best results when used fresh, so only small quantities should be bought, although it can be successfully frozen. Usually fresh yeast is blended with the liquid and left to activate then added to the dry ingredients.

Dried yeast – There are three types of this currently available:-

1. **The traditional dried yeast** usually sold in small tins. This is blended with the liquid first to activate it and left for 15 minutes, until it is frothy on top, before adding to the dry ingredients.

2. **The fast action yeast** which only needs one proving.

3. **The easy blend dried yeast** which is very fine granules and is added to the dry ingredients before the liquid. It will not work if added to the liquid first. It comes in sachets that are equivalent to 15 g (½ oz) ordinary dried yeast or 25 g (1 oz) fresh yeast.
We have used the easy blend dried yeast throughout our recipes because it is now so easily available, but if you wish to use any of the other types use the method associated with them.
In most of the recipes we have used strong plain flour because this absorbs more liquid and gives a better rise and nicer crust. Salt is necessary both for flavour and to prevent the bread from rising too quickly and spoiling the texture, so do not miss it out.

Steps for Successful Yeast Baking

Make sure that the ingredients and utensils are at room temperature not straight from the fridge or cool larder. After adding the liquid to the dry ingredients, knead. This is easiest done in a mixer with a dough hook, but it is immensely satisfying to do by hand, especially if you are in a bad mood and need to take out some aggression on something! The kneading should be continued until the dough is smooth and no longer sticky. The dough should then be put to prove or rise. If no warm airing cupboard is available one of the most successful ways to prove the bread is to put it in a polythene bag which has had 15 ml (1 tbsp) oil rubbed in it. Just tuck the opening under, but do not seal it. Put the bag containing the dough either in the microwave on HIGH power for just 10 seconds to get it started or put it in a fan oven set at 30°C and leave it until the dough has doubled in size. Do not try to rush this stage – it will take between 20 and 40 minutes and the bread will be much better for a good proving. You can do this overnight in a refrigerator, but be sure to let the dough come back to room temperature before shaping it.
The second kneading or knocking back is much lighter than the first and should only take two minutes. It helps to give a good texture and makes it easy to shape the bread. Prove or rise the shaped dough again until it has doubled in size, then brush with egg or glaze as directed in the recipe.

Baking
This should be done in a preheated oven. This is most important, otherwise the yeast will keep on growing and the shape will be spoilt. The LOW power microwave should be put on when the bread goes in. The bread is cooked when it is well risen and golden brown and should sound hollow when tapped on the bottom. If you think it needs a little more time, return the bread to the oven without its cooking dish and cook on conventional only.

WHITE BREAD

Makes 3 loaves

750 g (1½ lb) strong plain flour
5 ml (1 level tsp) salt
50 g (2 oz) margarine
1 sachet easy blend dried yeast
400 ml (¾ pt) warm water

1. Sieve the flour and salt together and rub in the margarine.

2. Add the dried yeast mix.

3. Add the liquid, stir in and turn onto a floured board. Knead for 5 minutes until it is smooth and elastic. Alternatively a dough hook or a mixer is very successful.

4. Put the dough into an oiled plastic bag and leave to rise until it has doubled in size. This can be done in your oven at about 30°C.

5. Turn the dough out and knead again well.

6. Divide the dough into 3 and shape into loaves, put into greased loaf dishes on a greased baking tray suitable for you oven.

7. Prove the bread again until it has doubled in size. Brush with milk or beaten egg.

8. Bake in a preheated oven at 220°C, LOW power microwave for 16–20 minutes or until golden brown and hollow sounding when tapped on the base.

—— VARIATION ——

For wholemeal bread use half wholemeal flour and half strong plain flour, which gives a delicious light loaf. Another variation would be to substitute some granary flour to give a more crunchy rough texture bread. The method is exactly the same as for white bread.

MILK BREAD

This is a richer slightly yellow bread. It is almost scone like and is delicious served warm at tea time with lashings of homemade jam. Clotted or whipped cream makes it all the more special.

Makes 2 loaves

450 g (1 lb) strong plain flour	
10 ml (2 level tsp) salt	
25 g (1 oz) lard	
1 sachet easy blend dried yeast	
300 ml (½ pt) tepid milk	

1. Sieve the flour and salt into a bowl and rub in the fat. Mix in the yeast, then stir in the warm milk and knead to a soft dough.

2. Knead on a floured surface for 5 minutes or until smooth and elastic in texture. Place the dough in an oiled plastic bag and leave to prove until doubled in size.

3. Knead again for 2 minutes, then divide into 2 and

shape into loaves. Leave to prove again until well risen, then brush with milk or a beaten egg and bake in a preheated oven at 200°C, LOW power microwave for 15–20 minutes.

—— COOK'S TIP ——

Add a little grated cheese or mixed herbs to the bread for a savoury loaf.

FRUIT BRAN TEABREAD

This is a recipe we have been making for years and it probably originally came from the back of a cereal packet. Having always made it using cups as a measure we give you these, as well as the traditional measures.

Makes 1 loaf

100 g (4 oz) Albran	2 cups
150 g (6 oz) caster sugar	1 cup
350 g (12 oz) dried fruit	2 cups
300 ml (½ pt) milk	
5 ml (1 level tsp) mixed spice	
100 g (4 oz) self raising flour	1 cup

1. Mix the Albran, sugar, fruit, spice and milk together. Leave for 2 hours or overnight.

2. Add the flour and mix well. Spoon into a greased 1 kg (2 lb) loaf dish.

3. Bake in a preheated oven at 200°C, LOW power microwave for 30–35 minutes or until a skewer comes out clean.

SWEET TWIST

A very attractive and extremely light sweet bread. The dough is almost batter-like and a little sticky to handle, so flour the hands lightly before kneading. The bread freezes very successfully. Add spices or fruit to the twist, if desired.

Makes 1 × 20 cm (8 in) twist

225 g (8 oz) strong plain flour

1.3 ml (¼ tsp) salt

25 g (1 oz) lard

40 g (1½ oz) caster sugar

½ sachet easy blend dried yeast

150 ml (¼ pt) hand hot milk

1. Sieve the flour and salt into a bowl and rub in the fat. Stir in the sugar and yeast.

2. Stir in the milk and mix to a light dough. Cover and leave in a warm place until doubled in size.

3. Turn onto a floured surface and knead lightly, adding a little extra flour if necessary. Roll into a long sausage approximately 60–75 cm (2–2.6 in) in length.

4. Lightly grease a 20 cm (8 in) round dish and coil the bread into the base of it. Cover and leave to prove in a warm place for approximately 20–30 minutes.

5. Place the butter, sugar and honey in a bowl and microwave on HIGH power for 1 minute. Stir until the sugar has dissolved then brush over the bread.

6. Bake in a preheated oven at 200°C, LOW power microwave for 20 minutes or until golden brown all over.

7. Leave for a few minutes in the dish before turning onto a wire rack to cool.

SYRUP AND OAT BREAD

This is a not too sweet bread, it looks attractive with oats on the top and is quick and easy to cook in a combination oven. It can be cooked in a glass loaf dish or try it cooked in casserole dishes so that the shape is different.

Makes 2 loaves

550 g (1¼ lb) strong plain flour

100 g (4 oz) rolled oats

10 ml (2 level tsp) salt

25 g (1 oz) margarine

1 sachet easy blend dried yeast

150 g (6 oz) golden syrup

400 ml (¾ pt) warm water

1. Mix the flour, oats, salt and rub in the margarine.

2. Add the yeast and mix.

3. Warm the water and syrup together until just warm, add to the dry ingredients and mix until smooth and leaving the sides of the bowl, adding a little extra flour if necessary.

4. Put into an oiled plastic bag, tuck end over and leave to prove until double in size.

5. Knead the dough lightly again and divide into 2. Shape into loaves and put into greased loaf dishes or casseroles.

6. Leave to prove again until doubled in size. Brush with milk and sprinkle with some extra oats.

7. Bake in a preheated oven 220°C, LOW power microwave for 16–20 minutes or until golden brown and sounding hollow when tapped on the bottom.

CHALLAH

This is a Jewish bread traditionally used to welcome the Sabbath. The most characteristic shape of this beautiful shiny loaf is of a plait but done with 4 pieces of bread not 3. If you feel 4 would be too complicated just make an ordinary plait, taking care that the middle of each roll is quite thick, tapering to thinner ends.

Makes 1 loaf

350 g (¾ lb) strong plain flour

5 ml (1 level tsp) salt

1 sachet of easy blend dried yeast

15 g (½ oz) sugar

200 ml (6 fl oz) warm water

2 eggs

25 g (1 oz) butter, melted

To glaze

1 egg yolk

15 ml (1 tbsp) water

1. Put the flour, salt, yeast and sugar in a bowl and mix.

2. Mix the water, melted butter and 2 eggs and add to the flour, beat well until incorporated, smooth and leaving the sides of the bowl. It should be fairly soft; if too dry add a little extra water or if too wet a little extra flour.

3. Put the dough in an oiled plastic bag and prove until doubled in size.

4. Turn the dough out and knead it for a couple of minutes. Divide into 3 or 4 equal portions, roll out into a sausage shape 1.5 cm (½ in) at each end and 3.5 cm (1½ in) in the centre. Plait.

5. Put into a greased glass baking tray and leave until doubled in size.

6. Mix together the egg yolk and water and brush the loaf well with it.

7. Bake the loaf in a preheated oven at 200°C, LOW power microwave for 20 minutes until golden brown and hollow sounding when tapped on the base. Cool on a wire rack.

LARDY CAKE

This is a very fattening cake but delicious. We make it now from a polyunsaturated white fat, instead of lard and pretend it is not increasing our waistline!

Makes 1 20×27.5 cm (8×11 in) cake

450 g (1 lb) strong plain flour

150 g (5 oz) white fat

10 ml (2 level tsp) salt

1 sachet easy blend dried yeast

300 ml (½ pt) tepid water

100 g (4 oz) caster sugar

5 ml (1 level tsp) mixed spice

100 g (4 oz) mixed dried fruit

15 ml (1 level tbsp) caster sugar plus 15 ml (1 tbsp) water

1. Sieve the flour and salt into a bowl, then rub in 25 g (1 oz) fat. Add the yeast, then stir in the water.

2. Knead the dough for 5 minutes (a mixer is fine), then put it into an oiled plastic bag to prove until it has doubled in size.

3. Roll the dough out of a large oblong, spread with ⅓ of the remaining fat and ⅓ of the sugar and spice.

4. Fold the dough into 3; seal the edges with the rolling pin.

5. Repeat steps 3 and 4.

6. Roll the dough out again to a large rectangle, spread with the remaining fat, sugar and dried fruit. Fold the dough into 3 and seal the edges with the rolling pin.

7. Put into a greased dish approximately 20×27.5 cm (8×11 in) and cook in a preheated oven at 220°C, LOW power microwave for 16 minutes then brush with the sugar solution.

SELKIRK BANNOCK

This is a teatime favourite now with both our families! The bannock originated from a baker in Selkirk and was apparently a firm favourite with Queen Victoria, when visiting the area. In olden days the bannock was served at every meal in some Scottish houses, warm at breakfast, with cheese at lunch and buttered for tea. The bannock should always be served in slices, not wedges.

Makes 1 × 20 cm (8 in) round

225 g (8 oz) strong plain flour

pinch of salt

25 g (1 oz) lard

100 g (4 oz) butter

50 g (2 oz) currants

50 g (2 oz) sultanas

50 g (2 oz) mixed peel

½ sachet easy blend dried yeast, ½ sachet fast acting dried yeast

150 ml (¼ pt) hand hot milk

1. Sieve the flour and salt into a bowl then add the lard and butter cut up into small cubes. Rub in until the mixture resembles fine breadcrumbs.

2. Add all the remaining ingredients, lastly stirring in the milk. Knead lightly to a soft dough then knead on a floured surface for about 5 minutes. Place the dough in an oiled plastic bag and leave to prove until doubled in size.

3. Turn onto a floured surface and knead again gently, then shape into a 17.5 cm (7 in) round and place on a greased baking dish. Leave again in a warm place for 15–20 minutes, then bake in a preheated oven at 200°C, LOW power microwave for 20 minutes, or until golden brown on the top and base. Serve sliced with butter.

GUGELHUMPF

What a lovely name! In Germany you can buy special Gugelhumpf tins, which are fluted ring moulds. We have not yet discovered a fluted non metalic ring mould, so we substituted a plain pyrex ring mould. Although perhaps not quite as pretty as the Gugelhumpf mould, the result was still excellent.

Makes 1 × 20 cm (8 in) ring

knob of butter

15 g (½ oz) split almonds

175 g (6 oz) strong plain flour

pinch of salt

25 g (1 oz) caster sugar

½ sachet easy blend dried yeast

100 ml (3½ fl oz) hand hot milk

50 g (2 oz) butter, melted

2 eggs, lightly beaten

grated rind ½ lemon

50 g (2 oz) raisins

25 g (1 oz) currants

icing sugar

1. Melt the knob of butter in the ring mould on HIGH power in the microwave for a few seconds. Brush around the mould then sprinkle over the split almonds.

2. Sieve the flour and salt into a bowl. Add the sugar and yeast, then stir in the milk, butter and eggs and beat thoroughly for 5 minutes. Lastly, beat in the lemon rind, raisins and currants.

3. Cover and leave in a warm place until doubled in size, then beat again to knock out the air and spoon into the ring mould. Put in a warm place until well risen, then bake in a preheated oven at 200°C, LOW power microwave for 15–20 minutes.

4. Allow the Gugelhumpf to cool in the ring mould for 5 minutes before turning out and dusting with icing sugar.

—— COOK'S TIP ——
A few chopped almonds can be added to the mixture along with the fruit.

STOLLEN

This is a German Christmas cake and is delicious, looks lovely and is ideal as a Christmas present. Although fairly extravagant to make, it is well worth the effort. It should be pale in colour, so the quick cooking time in a combination oven is helpful. A stollen will keep in a cool place for about a month if wrapped.

Makes 2 loaves

450 g (1 lb) strong plain flour

40 g (1½ oz) vanilla sugar (or caster sugar and 5 ml [1 tsp] vanilla essence)

1 sachet easy blend dried yeast

150 ml (¼ pt) warm milk

1 large egg

75 g (3 oz) butter, melted

grated rind of lemon

100 g (4 oz) sultanas

75 g (3 oz) currants

15 ml (1 tbsp) brandy

75 g (3 oz) almonds, chopped

100 g (4 oz) mixed peel

Marzipan

150 g (6 oz) caster sugar

150 g (6 oz) ground almonds

30 ml (2 tbsp) rose water

1 egg yolk

Decoration

75 g (3 oz) butter, melted

100 g (4 oz) icing sugar

1. Put the flour, sugar and yeast in a bowl and mix.

2. Mix the milk, egg and melted butter together and add to the flour with the lemon rind. Beat well until smooth and leaving the sides of the bowl. Put into an oiled plastic bag and leave to prove until doubled in size.

3. Meanwhile, put the sultanas, currants and brandy together, stir and microwave on HIGH for 1 minute. Leave to cool.

4. Mix together the marzipan ingredients and make into 2 sausages about 4 cm (1½ in) thick.

5. When the dough has doubled, knead it again or use a dough hook and add to it the soaked sultanas and currants, the almonds and peel. Continue to knead until they are incorporated.

6. Divide the dough into 2 and roll each piece out to an oval about 1.25 cm (½ in) thick. With the rolling pin press a hollow down the centre and lay the marzipan roll in.

7. Fold the dough over and seal. Place each on a buttered baking dish and brush with some of·the melted butter. Leave to prove until doubled in size, which will take 45 minutes.

8. Bake in a preheated oven at 200°C, LOW power microwave for 20 minutes. Repeat with the other stollen.

9. Brush the cooked stollen with the remaining butter and dust thickly with icing sugar. Cool on a wire rack. If you have a combination oven large enough to put the two stollen on a single tray, they will take an extra 2 or 3 minutes (remember they will swell during cooking).

APPEL KUCHEN

A 'Kuchen' is a German bread which is soft and sweet and is usually baked with some sort of topping. The following recipe is for an apple and cinnamon topping which is delicious, but other favourites are honey and almond or 'streusal' topping which is like a crumble.

Makes 1×20 cm (8 in) cake

225 g (8 oz) strong plain flour

2.5 ml (½ tsp) salt

25 g (1 oz) sugar

½ sachet easy blend dried yeast

150 ml (¼ pt) hand hot milk

25·g (1 oz) butter, melted

1 egg, lightly beaten

50 g (2 oz) raisins

Topping

1 large eating apple

cinnamon

15 ml (1 tbsp) caster sugar

1. Sieve the flour and salt into a bowl and mix in the sugar and yeast. Stir in the egg, butter and milk and beat to a soft dough. Beat for several minutes, then cover and leave in a warm place, until doubled in size.

2. Knock back the dough on a floured surface to its original size, and work in the raisins. Knead lightly for a few minutes, then shape into a round and place in a greased 20 cm (8 in) cake dish.

3. Peel, core and thinly slice the apple, cutting the slices in half, then press them gently into the surface of the dough. Sprinkle with a little cinnamon and caster sugar. Then leave in a warm place until well risen.

4. Bake the Kuchen in a preheated oven at 200°C, LOW power microwave for 20–25 minutes or until golden brown. Leave for a few minutes in the dish before turning out. Eat warm or cold.

SAVARIN

This is a delicious special occasion sweet. It can be made well in advance and in fact benefits from being left until the next day. The combination oven makes it wonderfully light and spongy, as well as saving cooking time. Rum essence could be used but the result will not be as special.

Serves 6–8

225 g (8 oz) strong plain flour

2.5 ml (½ level tsp) salt

50 g (2 oz) caster sugar

1 sachet easy blend dried yeast

100 g (4 oz) butter

4 eggs

90 ml (6 tbsp) warm milk

Syrup

150 g (6 oz) honey

150 ml (¼ pt) water

150 ml (¼ pt) rum

210 ml (8 fl oz) double cream, whipped

100 g (4 oz) apricot jam, warmed and sieved

1. Mix the flour, salt, sugar and easy blend dried yeast together.

2. Half melt the butter for 1 minute on HIGH in the microwave. Mix in the eggs and milk.

3. In a mixer, pour the liquid into the dry ingredients and beat well for about 2 minutes.

4. Pour the batter into a well greased savarin mould or 20 cm (8 in) ring dish.

5. Cover and leave in a warm place to rise, until the dish is ¾ full. Remove cover.

6. Bake in a preheated oven at 200°C, LOW power microwave for 15–20 minutes.

7. Turn out carefully. Place on a serving dish whilst still warm.

8. Mix the warmed honey, rum and water together and pour over the savarin, slowly so it has time to absorb.

9. Brush all over with apricot jam.

10. Pipe a collar of cream around the base of the savarin before serving.

────── SERVING SUGGESTION ──────
Fill the centre with strawberries, for an extra special treat.

PRUNE AND ORANGE WHOLEMEAL BREAD

This bread is delicious served warm at breakfast time with a chunky orange marmalade. It is especially good if a granary type of flour can be used which gives a really nutty texture. A sultana and lemon bread can be made in the same way.

Makes 1×450 g (1 lb) loaf

450 g (1 lb) wholemeal bread flour
5 ml (1 level tsp) salt
25 g (1 oz) caster sugar
1 sachet easy blend dried yeast
300 ml (½ pt) hand hot water
50 g (2 oz) dried prunes, stoned and chopped
grated rind of 1 orange

To glaze

milk or beaten egg

1. Place the flour, salt, caster sugar and yeast in a bowl and mix together. Stir in the water and knead together.

2. Knead the dough on a floured surface for 5 minutes, then place in an oiled plastic bag and leave in a warm place to rise until doubled in size.

3. Knock the dough back to its original size and work in the prunes and orange rind. Knead for a few minutes, then shape into a loaf, put on a greased baking dish and leave in a warm place until well risen.

4. Brush with the milk or beaten egg and cook in a preheated oven at 200°C, LOW power microwave for approximately 20 minutes or until brown and hollow sounding when tapped on the base.

APRICOT AND ALMOND BREAD

This is a coffee-coloured bread full of the flavour of apricots, especially delicious served with butter and a good apricot jam. The mixture of brown and white flour keeps the bread light.

Makes 1×450 g (1 lb) loaf

225 g (8 oz) strong brown flour
100 g (4 oz) strong plain flour
2.5 ml (½ tsp) salt
10 ml (2 level tsp) caster sugar
1 packet easy blend dried yeast
250 ml (9 fl oz) hand hot water
100 g (4 oz) dried apricots, chopped
25 g (1 oz) blanched almonds, chopped
milk or beaten egg to glaze

1. Sieve the flour and salt into a bowl, then mix in the sugar and yeast. Stir in the water and knead together. Knead lightly for 5 minutes, then place in an oiled plastic bag to prove until double in size.

2. Work the apricots and almonds into the dough and knead lightly for a few minutes, then shape into a loaf and place on a greased baking dish. Leave in a warm place for 15–20 minutes or until well risen.

3. Brush the loaf with milk or a beaten egg and bake in a preheated oven at 200°C, LOW power microwave for 15 minutes or until brown and hollow sounding.

────── COOK'S TIP ──────
Try not to leave too many apricots and almonds protruding from the top of the loaf as they tend to burn slightly during cooking

FRUIT MALT LOAF

This makes two of those moist sticky loaves that are wonderful, spread with butter for tea. If there is any left over they are great toasted for breakfast. This loaf also does you a power of good with lots of trace elements and minerals in the treacle, including iron, and wholemeal flour and raisins for fibre. Its a shame about the calories. Never mind just enjoy it!

Makes 2 loaves

200 g (8 oz) wholemeal flour
200 g (8 oz) strong plain flour
25 g (1 oz) margarine
150 g (6 oz) sultanas
1 sachet easy blend dried yeast
40 ml (2 rounded tbsp) malt extract
20 ml (1 rounded tbsp) black treacle
200 ml (8 fl oz) warm water
15 ml (1 tbsp) water
50 g (2 oz) sugar

1. Put the flour in a bowl, rub in the margarine and stir in the sultanas. Add the yeast dry.

2. Add the malt and treacle and warm water and with a dough hook knead until the mixture leaves the sides of the bowl.

3. Shape the dough into two loaves and place on a greased glass baking sheet.

4. Prove in a warm place until the loaves have doubled in size.

5. Melt the sugar in the water and microwave on HIGH for 1 minute. Brush the loaves with the syrup.

6. Preheat the oven to 220°C and cook the loaves on LOW power for 16–20 minutes or until they sound hollow when tapped on the bottom.

7. Brush the loaves again with the syrup. Resist the urge to cut until cool otherwise you will drag down the fruit.

TOMATO AND HERB BREAD

This is a cheerful coloured bread, delicious with soup or cheese. The aroma alone is enough to get everyone into the kitchen, waiting for it to come out of the oven, which will not take long.

Makes 2 loaves

700 g (1½ lb) strong plain flour
5 ml (1 level tsp) salt
50 g (2 oz) soft margarine
5 ml (1 level tsp) dried herbs
1 sachet easy blend dried yeast
60 ml (4 level tbsp) parmesan cheese, grated
20 ml (4 tsp) tomato puree
475 ml (15 fl oz) tepid water

1. Rub the margarine into the flour and salt.

2. Add the herbs, the sachet of dried yeast and 45 ml (3 level tbsp) of the parmesan cheese. Mix well.

3. Add the tomato puree and water, mixed together and knead the mixture well for about 4 minutes. A mixer with a dough hook helps.

4. Place the dough in an oiled plastic bag to prove until it has doubled in size.

5. Knock the dough back and knead again for a minute.

6. Shape into 2 loaves and either place in a loaf dish or put on a baking sheet. Prove again until double in size. Brush with milk and sprinkle with the remaining parmesan.

7. Bake in a preheated oven at 220°C, LOW power microwave for 15–20 minutes. It should sound hollow when knocked on the bottom.

See photograph page 45

WHOLEMEAL CHEESE CROWN

This is another successful yeast recipe. An alternative title would be Ploughman's Roll, all it needs is pickle and some extra cheese or salad. A pint would be welcome as well!
If you want to use only white flour this works perfectly – use 700 g (1½ lb) and follow the directions below.

Makes 2 crowns

450 g (1 lb) wholemeal flour
250 g (9 oz) strong plain flour
10 ml (2 level tsp) salt
1 sachet easy blend dried yeast
225 g (½ lb) strong cheddar cheese

1. Mix the flour, salt and yeast together.

2. Add 420 ml (¾ pt) warm water and knead until the dough leaves the sides of the bowl and is smooth and elastic.

3. Put into an oiled bag in a warm place to prove; or place in the microwave on HIGH power for 15 seconds.

4. When the dough has doubled in size knead again. Divide in half and each half into 8 pieces.

5. Cut the cheese into 16 pieces and put each piece into the centre of the divided dough. Shape into a roll enclosing the cheese completely.

6. Arrange 7 rolls in a loose circle on a greased glass baking sheet; put one in the centre allowing room to prove. Repeat with the rest.

7. Put in a warm place to prove. Damp the tops and dust with wholemeal flour.

8. Bake in a preheated oven at 220°C, LOW power microwave for 16–20 minutes.

—— VARIATION ——
Use half the dough to make a wholemeal loaf and half to make the cheese crown. Try using other cheese.

See photograph page 65

CHEESE TOPPED BACON AND ONION BREAD

We make this bread quite often either using the traditional recipe already given or, if in a hurry, a packet bread mix which is also excellent. This is so quick and easy enough to make for a lunch to serve with a homemade soup or even (dare we say it) a packet or canned soup that you have 'pepped' up with a little alcohol or cream.
People love the aroma of homemade bread and guests will think you have slaved away for hours especially for them. Do not let them into the secret!

Makes 2 loaves

50 g (2 oz) streaky bacon, derinded and chopped small
50 g (2 oz) onion, finely chopped
550 g (1 lb 4 oz) packet of bread mix
a little milk for brushing
75 g (3 oz) grated cheese

1. Place the bacon and onion in a casserole dish and microwave on HIGH for 3 minutes stirring once.

2. Make the bread mix up following the instructions on the packet.

3. Knead the bacon and onions and shape into 2 French loaf shapes.

4. Prove following the packet instructions.

5. Brush with milk and sprinkle with cheese.

6. Bake in a preheated oven 200°C, LOW power microwave for 16–20 minutes until golden.

See photograph page 25

SAVOURY MINCE STUFFED LOAF

This is such a surprise – you put a beautiful loaf of bread on the table and just when everyone begins to feel that's all they are getting for lunch you cut it into segments and lovely meat filling oozes out. Its delicious hot but almost better cold when the juices have soaked into the bread. Ideal for picnics just served with salad.

Serves 4–6

350 g (¾ lb) strong plain flour
5 ml (1 level tsp) salt
50 g (1 oz) margarine
½ sachet easy blend dried yeast
200 ml (⅜ pt) warm water

Filling

30 ml (2 tbsp) oil
1 large leek, finely sliced
225 g (8 oz) minced pork
salt and pepper
egg for glazing

1. Put the flour and salt in a bowl. Rub in the margarine and then add the yeast.

2. Add the water and mix until smooth and leaving the sides of the bowl.

3. Place the dough in an oiled plastic bag and leave to prove until doubled in size.

4. Meanwhile, put the oil in a casserole, add the leek and cook on HIGH power for 3 minutes. Stir well, add the pork and stir to break up. Microwave on HIGH power for 4 minutes, stir again and season well.

5. Knead the dough well, divide into 3, one piece will be the top and two the base. Grease a 20 cm (8 in) flan dish.

6. Knead two pieces together and roll out to fit the dish going well up the sides. Fill with the meat mixture.

7. Knead the other piece and damping the edges stick on the top of the meat, sealing the edges well. Snip some holes in the top and leave to prove for 20 minutes.

8. Brush the loaf with the beaten egg and bake in a preheated oven at 210°C, LOW power microwave for 20 minutes. Remove from the dish and leave to cool on a wire.

—— **VARIATION** ——
Ginger and spring onion loaf
Try a bunch of spring onions chopped with 225 g (8 oz) beef mince and 5 ml (1 level tsp) of grated fresh ginger as a filling instead.

CHELSEA BUNS

This is a very traditional English recipe, cooked in an untraditional way. The result is much less hit and miss because the dough is lovely and light when cooked in a combination oven. The quantity is for 1 sachet of easy blend yeast but if you wish to make less, halve the ingredients. In this recipe microwave the dried fruit with water; this plumps the fruit up and prevents burnt fruit on the top of the buns. You may wish to try this tip in other recipes where dried fruit is used.

Makes 16

450 g (1 lb) strong plain flour
5 ml (1 level tsp) salt
50 g (2 oz) caster sugar
50 g (2 oz) soft margarine
1 sachet easy blend dried yeast
150 ml (5 fl oz) warm milk
1 egg
75 g (3 oz) butter, melted
225 g (8 oz) mixed dried fruit including peel
45 ml (3 tbsp) water
125 g (4 oz) soft brown sugar
5 ml (1 level tsp) cinnamon
30 ml (2 tbsp) honey

1. Put the flour, salt and caster sugar in a large bowl, rub in the margarine, add the yeast.

2. Make the milk and beaten egg up to 300 ml (½ pt) and add to the flour mixture. Knead well until smooth and leaving the side of the bowl.

3. Put the dough into an oiled plastic bag and leave to prove until doubled in size.

4. Put the dried fruit and water in a bowl and microwave on HIGH for 2 minutes, stir well and leave to cool before draining well.

5. Knead the proved dough gently and roll out to an oblong 40 by 25 cm (16 by 10 in).

6. Brush the dough with the butter. Sprinkle with the cinnamon, sugar and well drained fruit, and roll up long edge towards long edge.

7. Cut the roll in 2.5 cm (1 in) slices and arrange in 2 greased 22.5 cm (9 in) cake dishes, leaving space to rise.

8. Leave to prove until doubled in size then bake in a preheated oven at 200°C, LOW power microwave for 20 minutes each.

9. Melt the honey for 1 minute on HIGH power and use to brush the warm buns.

HOT CROSS BUNS

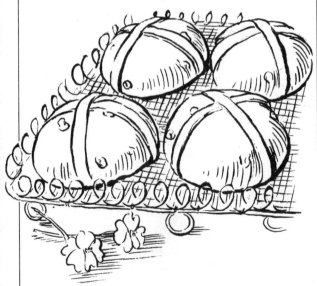

It is always fun to serve these traditional Easter buns hot from the oven. The use of an easy blend dried yeast and the combination oven makes them quick to prepare. They freeze very successfully, so can be made before Eastertide and warmed in the oven before serving. Instead of the pastry cross, a cross can be cut in the top of each bun with a sharp knife, before proving and baking.

Makes 12 buns

450 g (1 lb) strong plain flour

pinch of salt

75 g (3 oz) caster sugar

5 ml (1 level tsp) cinnamon

5 ml (1 level tsp) nutmeg

1 sachet easy blend dried yeast

50 g (2 oz) butter, melted

1 egg, beaten

150 ml (¼ pt) hand hot milk

50 g (2 oz) currants

25 g (1 oz) mixed peel, chopped

50 g (2 oz) softcrust pastry trimmings

To glaze

30 ml (2 level tbsp) caster sugar

15 ml (1 tbsp) water

1. Sieve the flour and salt into a bowl then add the sugar, cinnamon, nutmeg, yeast, currants and mixed peel.

2. Stir in the butter, egg and milk, then knead lightly to a smooth dough. Place in an oiled plastic bag and leave to prove until doubled in size.

3. When risen, knead the dough lightly then divide into 12, shape into balls and place on a greased baking dish, flattening the tops slightly.

4. Roll out the pastry trimmings and cut into strips, brush one side with water, then use to make a cross on each bun. Leave to rise again in a warm place for 15–20 minutes, then bake in a preheated oven at 220°C, LOW power microwave for 12–15 minutes.

5. To make the glaze, place the sugar and water in a small bowl and heat in the microwave on HIGH power for 1–2 minutes. Stir, then brush over the still warm buns. Serve warm.

Cakes and Biscuits

Cakes cooked in a microwave have had their attractions, in that they are very light and have extremely fast cooking times. However, their rather insipid appearance has been disappointing and has necessitated careful decoration or the use of coloured ingredients (eg. brown sugar, cocoa powder, dark spices etc). Their keeping qualities have also left much to be desired, although a virtually instant cake for the unexpected guest is always an advantage. Used on combination, your oven will produce light moist cakes with a traditional crust which you will not be ashamed to bring out of the cake tin. Pastry cooked in a microwave has always been poor however, with its pale appearance and tough texture. Cooked on combination, pastry will be light and golden, and even better than if it had been cooked in a traditional oven. Biscuits do not usually benefit from cooking in a combination oven due to their fast cooking times. The exception are shortbread type biscuits.

How to tell when cakes are cooked

Unlike microwave cooking, where cakes should be removed from the microwave whilst slightly wet on top, for the combination oven use the traditional test:-

1. The cake should have shrunk away slightly from the sides of the dish.

2. A warm skewer inserted in the centre should come out clean.

3. For sponge cakes press the top lightly with your finger and it should spring back.

CARIBBEAN CHERRY CAKE

This cake is packed with cherries and flavoured with coconut and rum – a delicious mixture with less than half the normal cooking time when cooked in the combination oven. For a darker cake use a dark soft brown sugar in place of the caster sugar.

Makes 1 × 20 cm (8 in) cake

175 g (6 oz) butter
175 g (6 oz) caster sugar
2 large eggs
150 ml (¼ pt) milk
30 ml (2 tbsp) rum
350 g (12 oz) self raising flour
275 g (10 oz) glace cherries
50 g (2 oz) desiccated coconut

1. Soften the butter slightly on a LOW power level in the microwave, then place in a bowl with the sugar and beat until pale and creamy.

2. Beat in the eggs, one at a time then gradually beat in the milk and rum. Sift in the flour and beat until smooth.

3. Halve the glace cherries then coat in the coconut and stir into the cake mixture.

4. Spoon the mixture into a greased and bottom lined 20 cm (8 in) cake dish and bake in a preheated oven at 180°C, LOW power microwave for 30 minutes. Leave to cool for a short time in the dish before turning out onto a wire rack.

MADEIRA CAKE

If you wonder how the Madeira cake got its name when not a drop of alcohol is included in the recipes, it is because in days gone by, the cake would be served in 'upper class' houses, mid morning accompanied by a glass of Madeira. Enjoy it with or without the alcohol!

Serves 8

175 g (6 oz) butter or margarine
175 g (6 oz) caster sugar
3 large eggs
110 g (4 oz) plain flour
110 g (4 oz) self raising flour
grated rind and juice of ½ a large lemon
2 thin slices of citrus peel

1. Cream together the butter and sugar until light and fluffy, then beat in the eggs, one at a time.

2. Sieve the flours together and fold in along with the lemon rind and juice.

3. Grease and line the base of a 17.5 cm (7 in) cake dish with grease-proof paper.

4. Turn the mixture into the dish, making a slight hollow in the centre and arrange the citrus peel on top.

5. Bake in a preheated oven at 190°C, LOW power microwave for approximately 20 minutes or until golden brown and a skewer inserted into the middle comes out clean.

6. Allow the cake to cool in the dish for 5 minutes before turning out onto a wire rack.

VARIATION
The addition of lemon rind and juice sharpens the flavour of the cake, but milk can be added instead. For a seed cake 10 ml (2 level tsp) caraway seeds can be added with the flour. Omit the lemon and citrus peel.

DOUBLE CHOCOLATE CAKE

This is a particularly good chocolate cake recipe, lovely and moist and especially easy to make if you have a mixer. It has a hard chocolate icing and a soft chocolate butter cream filling so the contrast of textures is excellent. Freezes well and cooks extremely quickly.

Serves 8

Cake

100 g (4 oz) self raising flour

125 g (5 oz) caster sugar (vanilla sugar is best)
or 5 ml (1 tsp) vanilla essence

5 ml (1 level tsp) bicarbonate of soda

25 g (1 oz) cocoa

50 g (2 oz) butter, melted

150 ml (¼ pt) single cream

Butter cream

75 g (3 oz) butter

125 g (5 oz) icing sugar

15 g (½ oz) cocoa

15 ml (1 tbsp) cream or top of milk

Topping

225 g (8 oz) plain chocolate

8 almonds, toasted

1. Put all the cake ingredients in the mixing bowl and beat well with a mixer for 2 minutes.

2. Turn the mixture into a greased and base lined 20 cm (8 in) cake dish and bake in a preheated oven at 180°C, LOW power microwave for 16–18 minutes or until slightly shrunk from the sides. Turn out onto a wire rack to cool.

3. Combine all the ingredients for the butter cream and beat well until smooth.

4. Split the cake in half horizontally and sandwich with half the butter cream. Put the rest in a piping bag with a star nozzle.

5. Break the chocolate into pieces and place in a bowl in the microwave. Microwave on HIGH power for 4 minutes or until melted.

6. Spread the chocolate over the top of the cake and allow to harden; repeat if necessary.

7. Decorate the top with swirls of butter cream and the whole blanched almonds.

———— COOK'S TIP ————
Put the almonds on a plate and microwave on HIGH for a couple of minutes until brown.

See photograph page 101

CELEBRATION CAKE

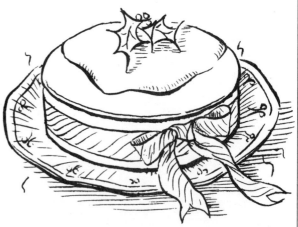

This is a wonderful cake recipe which has been used for many years at Christmas, christenings and weddings. It is especially useful because it is not a crumbly cake and is therefore very easy to cut (no crumbs all over the floor). We have used cake tins for this because cake dishes of the right size are not currently available. However, check with your manufacturer's handbook that metal is usable in your oven on combination before you go ahead. If you have to cook this cake purely in the conventional oven, we give you the normal timings. As you can see from the conventional timings this cake in the past has quite literally taken all day to cook. Now with the combination oven it is no longer a marathon to make and it only needs lining with one layer of grease-proof and no brown paper around the outside. If you like, after it has been cooked you can puncture the top with a skewer and pour in a little extra brandy. One last word, make this at least a month in advance to allow flavours to develop. In fact a cake tasted two and a half years after it was made was still wonderful.

Ingredients		METRIC	IMPERIAL	METRIC	IMPERIAL	METRIC	IMPERIAL
	round tin	15 cm	6 in	22.5 cm	9 in	28 cm	11 in
	square tin	13 cm	5 in	20 cm	8 in	26 cm	10½ in
butter		100 g	4 oz	275 g	10 oz	450 g	1 lb
dark soft brown sugar		100 g	4 oz	275 g	10 oz	450 g	1 lb
eggs size 2		2	2	5	5	9	9
plain flour		125 g	5 oz	400 g	14 oz	550 g	1¼ lb
mixed spice		2.5 ml	½ tsp	5 ml	1 tsp	10 ml	2 tsp
mixed dried fruit & peel		400 g	14 oz	1.050 kg	2 lb 6 oz	1.625 kg	3 lb 10 oz
almonds halved		50 g	2 oz	75 g	3 oz	150 g	6 oz
cherries		50 g	2 oz	75 g	3 oz	150 g	6 oz
black treacle		15 ml	1 tbsp	30 ml	2 tbsp	45 ml	3 tbsp
brandy		15 ml	1 tbsp	45 ml	3 tbsp	75 ml	5 tbsp

COOKING BY COMBINATION

Tin preparation Grease and line with grease-proof paper

Temp	140°C		140°C		140°C	
Microwave power	low		low		low	
Cooking time	50 min–1 hr 20 min		1 hr 15 min–2 hr 10 min		1 hr 30 min–2 hr 30 min (will not fit in ovens with turntables)	

Timings in your oven

Check 5 minutes before the end by inserting a skewer into the centre; it should come out clean when the cake is done.

Cooking by conventional only

Tin preparation Grease and line tins with 3 layers of grease-proof paper and tie double thickness of brown paper around the outside of the tin.

	round tin	15 cm	6 in	22.5 cm	9 in	28 cm	11 in
	square tin	13 cm	5 in	20 cm	8 in	26 cm	10½ in
Temp		140°C		140°C		130°C	
Cooking time		2½–3 hr 15 min		4–5½ hr		5–6½ hr	

Timings in your oven

Check 10 minutes before the end by inserting a skewer into the centre; it should come out clean when the cake is done.

1. Grease and line the tins with grease-proof paper.

2. Cream the fat and sugar until it is soft and creamy. Beat in the eggs one at a time.

3. Add the sifted flour with the rest of the ingredients, mix well. The mixture should be quite stiff.

4. Transfer to the tins and hollow out the centre slightly. Cook for the times on the chart.

NB You will notice there is quite a wide variation in timings when combination or conventional are used. This is due to the long cooking times and the different systems used by various manufacturers. Keep checking your cake after the minimum time is reached; you will not harm the cake by opening the door. Once you have cooked the cakes fill in the timings in the space left on the chart for your future reference.

DUNDEE CAKE

This is one of the most traditional of British cake recipes, with its characteristic decoration of split almonds on top. No high tea is complete without one. This is a particularly nice recipe with the addition of orange. It keeps beautifully, if you give it the chance.

Serves 10

225 g (8 oz) butter

225 g (8 oz) soft sugar

4 eggs

300 g (11 oz) plain flour

5 ml (1 level tsp) baking powder

2.5 ml (½ tsp) mixed spice

grated rind of an orange plus 30 ml (2 tbsp) of the juice

225 g (8 oz) currants

225 g (8 oz) sultanas

150 g (6 oz) raisins

100 g (4 oz) mixed peel

100 g (4 oz) glace cherries, halved

25 g (1 oz) almonds, chopped

25 g (1 oz) split almonds

1. Cream the butter and sugar until light and fluffy.

2. Gradually beat in the eggs, then add the flour, baking powder and spice sieved together.

3. Add all the other ingredients except the split almonds. Mix gently but thoroughly.

4. Pile the mixture into a greased and base lined 20 cm (8 in) cake dish. Smooth the top and arrange the split almonds on it.

5. Bake in a preheated oven at 180°C for 45 minutes. Pierce with a skewer to see if it is cooked – it should come out clean.

YORKSHIRE PARKIN

This is an old family recipe which came from Yorkshire bringing back memories of childhood teas when it was always on the menu. Do not worry if the Parkin sinks a little in the middle – this is quite normal. A little less flour and a little more oatmeal can be used for a coarser texture.

Makes 12 squares

350 g (12 oz) plain flour

10 ml (2 level tsp) ground ginger

10 ml (2 level tsp) baking powder

5 ml (1 level tsp) bicarbonate of soda

100 g (4 oz) lard

225 g (8 oz) dark soft brown sugar

50 g (2 oz) medium oatmeal

100 g (4 oz) black treacle

100 g (4 oz) golden syrup

300 ml (½ pt) milk

1. Sieve the flour, ginger, baking powder and bicarbonate of soda into a bowl. Cut the fat into small pieces and rub into the flour until the mixture resembles fine breadcrumbs.

2. Add the sugar and oatmeal, then warm the treacle and syrup and stir into the mixture with the milk. Beat until smooth.

3. Grease a 25×25 cm (9×9 in) or 20×30 cm (8×10 in) dish and line the base with grease-proof paper. Turn the mixture into the dish and bake in a preheated oven at 190°C, LOW power microwave for 18–20 minutes.

4. Leave to cool in the dish for 5 minutes, before turning out and cooling on a rack. Wrap in foil when cold and store for 1 week before eating.

PASSION CAKE

Carrot cake is the rather less appetising name for this recipe. No one really knows how the name 'Passion cake' developed, although the cake is sometimes decorated with passion fruit. It is a beautifully moist cake which cooks extremely well in the combination oven.

Serves 8

225 g (8 oz) caster sugar
175 g (6 oz) soft margarine
2 eggs
5 ml (1 tsp) vanilla essence
175 g (6 oz) self raising flour
2.5 ml (½ tsp) baking powder
5 ml (1 level tsp) cinnamon
225 g (8 oz) carrots, peeled and finely grated

Icing

50 g (2 oz) cream cheese
75 ml (2½ fl oz) double cream
100 g (4 oz) icing sugar
15 ml (1 tbsp) lemon juice

1. Place all the cake ingredients together in a bowl and beat until smooth and creamy.

2. Grease and line the base of a 20 cm (8 in) cake dish with grease-proof paper.

3. Turn the mixture into the dish and bake in a preheated oven at 200°C, MEDIUM power microwave for approximately 20 minutes or until golden brown and a skewer inserted into the middle comes out clean.

4. Leave the cake in the dish for 5 minutes, before turning out onto a wire rack to cool.

5. To make the icing, beat the cream cheese until soft. Whisk the cream until beginning to thicken then add to the cream cheese. Gradually mix in the sifted icing sugar and lemon juice. Spread over the top of the cake.

—— V A R I A T I O N ——

Make a larger quantity of less sweet icing sugar by using more double cream. Use to fill and top the cake and decorate with sliced passion fruit. This turns the cake into a gateaux.

GINGER BREAD

A useful tip when suffering from early pregnancy queeziness is to eat ginger in any form! It really does work and even seems to be good for travel sickness. Consequently, this is not only a delicious tea time treat, but can also have medicinal qualities too. For a honey and ginger bread, substitute honey for the golden syrup.

Makes 1 × 20 cm (8 in) square

450 g (1 lb) plain flour
15 ml (1 level tbsp) dried ginger
15 ml (1 level tbsp) baking powder
175 g (6 oz) black treacle
175 g (6 oz) golden syrup
175 g (6 oz) butter
225 g (8 oz) demerara sugar

1. Sieve the flour, ginger and baking powder into a mixing bowl.

2. Place the treacle, syrup, butter and sugar into a bowl and heat on HIGH power for 4 minutes. Stir to dissolve the sugar, then pour over the flour and beat together thoroughly.

3. Grease and line the base of a 20 cm (8 in) square dish with grease-proof paper. Pour in the mixture and bake in a preheated oven at 180°C, LOW power microwave for 20–25 minutes.

VICTORIA SPONGE

Although not quite as brown as a traditional sponge, the speed with which this is cooked and the lightness of texture make it well worthwhile. For variations, see alternatives at the end of the recipe.

Makes 1×20 cm (8 in) cake

175 g (6 oz) margarine or butter
175 g (6 oz) caster sugar
3 eggs
175 g (6 oz) self raising flour
30 ml (2 tbsp) milk

To finish

jam
icing sugar

1. If the margarine or butter is hard, soften on a LOW power level in the microwave, then place with all the remaining ingredients in a bowl and beat until smooth and creamy.

2. Grease and line the base of a 20 cm (8 in) cake dish, then spoon in the cake mixture. Smooth over the top, making a slight hollow in the cake.

3. Bake in a preheated oven at 200°C, LOW power microwave for 15 minutes, or until a skewer comes out clean. Leave in the dish for 5–10 minutes, before turning out onto a cooling rack.

4. When cool, split in half, and fill with the jam. Sprinkle with sieved icing sugar.

—— VARIATION ——

For an orange or lemon cake, add the grated rind of the fruit and 30 ml (2 tbsp) of juice in place of the milk. Use the remaining juice to make glace icing to ice the cake. Fill with butter cream.

LEMON ALMOND CAKE

A really delicious plain cake for tea, it keeps well and is rather unusual because it does not have flour in it. The sharpness of the lemon icing really contrasts beautifully.

Serves 8

4 eggs, separated
175 g (7 oz) caster sugar
100 g (4 oz) ground almonds
90 g (3½ oz) semolina
grated rind and juice of ½ lemon

Glace icing

juice of ½ lemon
150 g (6 oz) icing sugar

1. Grease and base line a 22 cm (9 in) deep cake dish; sprinkle it with caster sugar.

2. Put the egg yolks and sugar in a mixer and beat until thick and white.

3. Add the almond and the rind and juice.

4. Beat the egg whites until stiff and fold them with the semolina into the almond mixture.

5. Turn the mixture into the cake dish and bake in an oven preheated to 180°C, LOW power microwave, for 16 minutes.

6. Cool the cake.

7. Cream the icing sugar with the lemon juice until smooth and spread the glace icing over the cake.

8. Decorate with a slice of lemon if required.

Left to right: Spicy coffee crumble cake (page 107); Kerst krans (page 109); Bakewell tart (page 113); Double chocolate cake (page 96).

OVERLEAF
Left to right: Sunday best apple pie (page 111); Queen of puddings (page 120); Walnut and coffee gateau with strawberries (page 103); Linzer torte (page 118).

SIMNEL CAKE

A traditional Easter cake, decorated with small balls of marzipan, one for each apostle. However its much too nice to keep for just once a year. There are two versions of this recipe, one where you bake a cake, split it and sandwich it with almond paste and the other where the almond paste is actually cooked in the cake. The latter is much the best version. Usually it takes 3 hours to cook but now in the combination oven about 45 minutes.

Serves 12

150 g (6 oz) butter
150 g (6 oz) caster sugar
3 eggs, beaten
150 g (6 oz) plain flour
5 ml (1 level tsp) mixed spice
550 g (1 lb 4 oz) mixed dried fruit including peel
50 g (2 oz) blanched almonds, chopped
50 g (2 oz) glace cherries
grated rind of half a lemon
30 ml (2 tbsp) milk
550 g (1 lb 4 oz) almond paste
little glace icing

1. Cream the butter and sugar together until light and fluffy; gradually add the eggs.

2. Add the flour, spice, fruit, nuts, cherries, lemon and milk and mix together carefully.

3. Transfer half the mixture to a greased and base lined 20 cm (8 in) cake dish.

4. Roll out 225 g (8 oz) of almond paste in a 18 cm (7 in) diameter circle, place it gently on top of the cake mixture and cover with the remaining mixture.

5. Bake in a preheated oven at 160°C, LOW power microwave for 45–50 minutes or until a skewer comes out clean.

6. Cool the cake on a wire rack.

7. When cool, roll out the remaining almond paste to 20 cm (8 in) diameter, cut a 7.5 cm (3 in) diameter circle from the centre and with this make twelve small balls.

8. Damp the underside of the almond paste and stick it to the top of the cake, arranging the balls around the top.

9. Grill under the hot grill until the almond paste has coloured. Watch it carefully so it does not burn.

10. Allow to cool and fill the centre hole on the top of the cake with a little Royal Icing.

DATE AND APPLE CAKE

This is a moist cake quickly cooked in the combination oven. During the autumn when apples are plentiful its very economical to make and is delicious served with pouring cream as a dessert if you find you cannot resist it while warm. For an Apple and Sultana cake, use sultanas instead of the dates.

Serves 8

225 g (9 oz) self raising flour
5 ml (1 level tsp) cinnamon
200 g (8 oz) caster sugar
100 g (4 oz) butter or margarine
100 g (4 oz) dates, chopped
275 g (10 oz) cooking apples, diced
2 eggs, beaten
60 ml (4 tbsp) milk

1. Mix the flour, cinnamon and sugar together. Rub in the butter.

2. Add the dates, apples, beaten eggs and milk. Mix together well.

3. Turn the mixture into a greased and base lined 20 cm (8 in) cake dish. Cook in a preheated oven 180°C, LOW power microwave for 28–30 minutes.

4. Leave to cool in the dish for 10 minutes before turning out.

5. Dust with icing sugar if desired.

Baked cheese cake (page 114) with Tarte aux poires (page 115).

GLACE FRUIT AND BANANA CAKE

Being an unusual cross between a fruit and banana cake, it has wide appeal, is fairly moist and is guaranteed to disappear very fast.

Serves 8

125 g (4 oz) soft margarine

125 g (4 oz) light brown sugar

2 eggs

15 ml (1 tbsp) golden syrup

225 g (8 oz) self raising flour

2.5 ml (½ tsp) mixed spice

350 g (12 oz) mashed bananas

100 g (4 oz) sultanas

50 g (2 oz) mixed peel

50 g (2 oz) glace cherries

50 g (2 oz) chopped walnuts

1. Cream the margarine and sugar in a mixer.

2. Beat in the eggs, add the golden syrup.

3. Fold in the flour, spice and all the other ingredients.

4. Grease and base line a 20 cm (8 in) cake dish. Bake in a preheated oven at 180°C, LOW power for 30 minutes.

BOILED FRUIT CAKE

A good fruit cake recipe is always useful. This recipe makes a large fairly economical one which can be eaten the same day although keeping it would not hurt and it freezes well.
One of the things we hate most about making cakes is lining tins and tying brown paper round the outside to prevent the cake from over cooking. Because the cooking time is so reduced – half an hour instead of two – the outside does not get time to over cook, so the brown paper is not necessary – one chore less to do.

Serves 12

175 g (6 oz) brown sugar

100 g (4 oz) margarine

300 ml (½ pt) milk

400 g (14 oz) mixed dried fruit

150 g (5 oz) glace cherries

50 g (2 oz) walnuts

5 ml (1 level tsp) mixed spice

2.5 ml (½ tsp) bicarbonate soda

350 g (12 oz) self raising flour

2 size 3 eggs, beaten

1. Put the margarine, sugar and milk together in a large bowl. Microwave on HIGH for 3 minutes.

2. Add the fruit, cherries, walnuts, spice and bicarbonate soda. Microwave on HIGH for 8 minutes, stirring once or twice.

3. Cool the mixture to blood heat and add the flour and beaten eggs.

4. Pour the mixture into a 20 cm (8 in) cake dish, greased and lined.

5. Preheat the oven, cook for 30 minutes at 180°C, LOW power microwave or until a skewer inserted in the centre comes out clean.

PINEAPPLE AND MARZIPAN CAKE

This is an unusual cake because it has marzipan cubes cooked in it with the pineapple. Delicious and only 25 minutes in your combination oven.

Serves 8

150 g (6 oz) caster sugar

150 g (6 oz) soft margarine

3 eggs, beaten

225 g (8 oz) plain flour

5 ml (1 level tsp) baking powder

150 g (6 oz) marzipan, diced

150 g (6 oz) pineapple pieces, well drained

1. Cream the sugar and margarine until white. Add the beaten eggs one at a time.

2. Sieve the flour and baking powder together and add to the creamed mixture with the rest of the ingredients. Mix gently.

3. Grease and base line a 20 cm (8 in) cake dish, turn the mixture into it and smooth the top.

4. Cook in a preheated oven at 190°C, LOW power microwave for 25–30 minutes or until golden.

SPICY COFFEE CRUMBLE CAKE

This is a really appetising cake, moist, attractive and lovely with coffee and rather unusual because it has cherries in it.

Serves 8

| 175 g (6 oz) soft margarine |
| 175 g (6 oz) soft brown sugar |
| 2 eggs |
| 15 ml (1 level tbsp) instant coffee |
| 5 ml (1 level tsp) mixed spice |
| 250 g (9 oz) self raising flour |
| 150 ml (¼ pt) milk |
| 125 g (4 oz) glace cherries, halved |

Topping

| 75 g (3 oz) flour |
| 5 ml (1 level tsp) mixed spice |
| 50 g (2 oz) demerara sugar |
| 40 g (1½ oz) butter |

1. Cream the margarine and sugar together until light and fluffy. Gradually beat in the eggs.

2. Add the coffee, spice, flour, milk and cherries. Stir until well mixed.

3. Turn the mixture into a 20 cm (8 in) cake dish, greased and base lined.

4. Mix the topping ingredients together, rubbing in the butter until it resembles breadcrumbs; sprinkle evenly over the cake.

5. Bake the cake in a preheated oven at 180°C, LOW power microwave for 35 minutes or until a skewer comes out clean from the centre.

6. Cool the cake for 15 minutes before removing from the dish.

See photograph page 101

LATTICE BISCUITS

These are a cross between a cake and a biscuit and look pretty dusted with icing sugar. They will not last long because the children love them. Do not be tempted to use poor quality jam; homemade is best of all.

Makes 16–20

| 100 g (4 oz) ground almonds |
| 225 g (8 oz) plain flour |
| 225 g (8 oz) caster sugar |
| 175 g (6 oz) butter |
| 5 ml (1 level tsp) cinnamon |
| 5 ml (1 level tsp) lemon rind, grated |
| 1 egg, beaten |
| 175 g (6 oz) strawberry or other quality jam |

1. Soften the butter and add all the other ingredients, except the jam. Beat well until thoroughly mixed into a dough.

2. Press half the dough into a greased 28×18 cm (11× 7 in) dish evenly. Spread the jam over.

3. Roll the remaining dough into pencil thickness ropes, lay these over the jam to form a lattice pattern.

4. Bake in a combination oven preheated to 180°C, LOW power microwave for 20 minutes.

5. Partly cool in the dish and cut into bars before completely cold.

6. Dust with icing sugar if required.

FRUIT AND COCONUT SLICE

A light spongy slice in spite of being made with wholemeal flour. It is a favourite in our home and is lovely still warm or cold in packed lunches.

Makes 12–14 slices

Topping

50 g (2 oz) apple, chopped

25 g (1 oz) butter

200 g (8 oz) dried fruit

grated rind and juice of an orange

2.5 ml (½ level tsp) mixed spice

2 eggs

100 g (4 oz) soft brown sugar

5 ml (1 tsp) vanilla essence

175 g (6 oz) dessicated coconut

15 ml (1 level tbsp) wholemeal flour

2.5 ml (½ level tsp) baking powder

Base

100 g (4 oz) soft margarine

50 g (2 oz) soft brown sugar

175 g (6 oz) wholemeal self raising flour

1. Mix the first five ingredients together in a casserole, cover and microwave on HIGH for 5 minutes.

2. Next make the base by creaming the butter and sugar together until light and fluffy. Stir in the self raising flour.

3. Press evenly over the base of 1 18×23 cm (7×9 in) dish greased, and base lined to make it easy to get out.

4. Now complete the topping by beating the eggs, sugar and vanilla together in a mixer until thick and creamy.

5. Stir in the cooled fruit, coconut baking powder and flour and spread over the base.

6. Bake at 190°C, LOW power microwave for 16–20 minutes or until golden brown.

HONEYED DATE AND WALNUT LOAF

This is a very quick teatime cake which is fairly crumbly but keeps well. It looks very attractive with glazed walnuts on the top. In the past this cake has taken an hour and a half to cook, now with the combination oven 20 minutes.

Serves 8

250 g (8 oz) wholemeal self raising flour

2.5 ml (½ level tsp) cinnamon

2.5 ml (½ level tsp) mixed spice

75 g (3 oz) soft margarine

50 g (2 oz) soft brown sugar

125 g (4 oz) honey

50 ml (12 fl oz) milk

1 egg

125 g (4 oz) dates, chopped

50 g (2 oz) walnuts, chopped

Optional for decoration

50 g (2 oz) walnuts, roughly chopped

50 g (2 oz) honey

1. Mix the flour, spice and sugar together. Rub in the margarine.

2. Warm the honey, on HIGH for 1 minute, mix it with the milk and egg.

3. Add the honey mixture, dates and walnuts to the flour, mix well.

4. Turn the mixture into a greased 13×22 cm (5½×9 in) cake dish and bake in a preheated oven at 180°C, LOW power microwave for 20 minutes.

5. Leave to cool for 20 minutes before turning out.

6. Put the honey for decoration in a cup with the walnuts. Microwave on HIGH for 1 minute. Spread over the top of the loaf.

VARIATION
To make an apricot and walnut cake use dried apricots instead of the dates but make sure they are of the ready soaked variety.

KERST KRANS

This is a traditional Dutch recipe cooked in the modern way. It looks very pretty when cooked just like a Christmas wreath, so it is a useful alternative for that time of the year. However the taste is good enough for all the year.

Serves 6

225 g (8 oz) puff pastry

225 g (8 oz) almond paste *or* 175 g (6 oz) ground almonds

120 g (4 oz) caster sugar

1 egg

juice of ½ lemon

almond essence

To glaze

1 egg, beaten

To decorate

Apricot jam

Glace cherries

Angelica

Chopped almonds

1. Roll out the pastry to an oblong 11×51 cm (4½×20 in).

2. If making your own almond paste, mix together all the ingredients and knead well.

3. Form the almond paste into a long sausage and place down the centre of the pastry.

4. Brush the edges of the pastry with beaten egg and fold over the almond paste. Seal the edges. Form into a ring and seal the ends together.

5. Place on a baking sheet and brush with beaten egg. Bake in a preheated oven at 220°C, LOW power microwave for 12–14 minutes, or until golden brown.

6. Soften a little jam on HIGH power in the microwave for 30 seconds and brush over the pastry. Decorate with glace cherries, angelica and chopped almonds.

See photograph page 101

SHORTBREAD

Shortbread, although delicious, takes too long to cook traditionally to make it an economic proposition. It can be cooked in a microwave on HIGH power only taking 4 minutes, but the result is slightly soggy. This is a wonderful combination, giving a crisp golden shortbread which can be knocked up in minutes for unexpected tea guests when the biscuit tin is bare.

Makes 1 round

125 g (4 oz) butter

150 g (5 oz) plain flour

25 g (1 oz) semolina or rice flour

50 g (2 oz) caster sugar

caster sugar to sprinkle over the shortbread

1. Place the butter in a mixing bowl and soften in the microwave on LOW power for 1 minute.

2. Beat in all the remaining ingredients and press into a greased 20 cm (8 in) round dish. Prick the shortbread thoroughly with a fork.

3. Bake in a preheated oven at 180°C, LOW power microwave for 12 minutes, turning the shortbread occasionally.

4. Cool in the dish slightly, then sprinkle with caster sugar and mark into wedges. When firm to the touch, remove from the dish and finish cooling on a wire rack.

------ VARIATION ------

To make Yorkshire 'Claggy Cake', cook the same quantity of shortbread in a slightly larger dish then top with caramel made from 75 g (3 oz) butter, 125 g (4 oz) caster sugar, 1 small tin of condensed milk and 30 ml (2 tbsp) golden syrup. Heat all the ingredients on HIGH power in the microwave for 3 minutes, then stir until the sugar has dissolved. Return to the microwave and cook on HIGH power for a further 4–5 minutes or until golden brown. Pour over the shortbread, once the caramel has set, spread with melted chocolate and cut into wedges. Very fattening but worth every calorie!

Hot and Cold Desserts

In this section we have given a selection of recipes, both traditional and new. Although perhaps some of the recipes are heavy in calories, all are light in time. In many the filling is cooked at the same time as the base or topping, cutting out one stage in the cooking process – for example, the fruit crumbles and the apple pie. Custards can be cooked without curdling or the use of a bain-marie and even the humble bread and butter pudding has a new lease of life when cooked in the combination oven.

SUNDAY BEST APPLE PIE

An apple pie always goes down well and this one is just that bit different. Putting the flour in the filling gives a pie that stays together. If there is any left over it is delicious cold.

Serves 6

Pastry

135 g (4½ oz) margarine and lard, mixed
225 g (8 oz) plain flour
35 g (1½ oz) caster sugar
1 egg
5 ml (1 tsp) lemon juice
60 ml (4 tbsp) water

Filling

675 g (1½ lb) cooking apples, peeled and cored
75 g (3 oz) brown sugar
25 g (1 oz) plain flour
rind and juice of 1 orange
50 g (2 oz) sultanas

1. Rub the fat into the flour until it resembles breadcrumbs.

2. Mix the sugar, egg and lemon juice together and add to the flour with the water to make a dough.

3. Knead gently on a floured surface and roll ⅔ out to line a 20 cm (8 in) pie dish.

4. For the filling, mix together the flour, sugar, spice, rind and sultanas.

5. Sprinkle a ⅓ of the filling over the base of the flan, add ½ the apples then another ⅓, then the rest of the apples and remaining ⅓. Add the juice.

6. Top with the remaining pastry.

7. Cook in a preheated oven at 200°C, LOW power microwave for 15–20 minutes.

See photograph page 102

TREASURE CHEST FLAN

The name for this flan came about after a local newspaper ran a competition to find a name for the recipe. The winner won a place on a course at the cookery school. It is fairly easy but substantial tart, lovely on a cool day. Serve it warm with either pouring cream or custard.

Serves 6

Base ingredients

175 g (6 oz) plain flour
5 ml (1 level tsp) baking powder
5 ml (1 level tsp) cinnamon
75 g (3 oz) margarine
75 g (3 oz) caster sugar
1 egg

Topping

100 g (4 oz) golden syrup
5 ml (1 level tsp) cinnamon
1 egg and a yolk
50 g (2 oz) dates, chopped
50 g (2 oz) walnuts, chopped
3 large cooking apples

1. Sieve flour, baking powder and cinnamon together and rub in the margarine.

2. Mix in the sugar and egg, press into a 20 cm (8 in) round cake dish pushing up the sides.

3. Warm the golden syrup in the microwave and beat in the cinnamon and egg.

4. Sprinkle the base of the tart with dates and walnuts. Peel, core and slice the apples and arrange onto the base, heaping it in the centre.

5. Carefully pour the topping over the apples. Bake in a preheated oven at 180°C, LOW power microwave for 16–20 minutes or until the custard is set.

PLUM TORTE

Our Suffolk garden is old and rambling, so it was with no surprise that last year we discovered two plum trees which we had not known were there. The branches were so heavily ladened with fruit that several of them had broken, so we set to work with enthusiasm, eating up the delicious fruit. After we had eaten our fill of fresh fruit, there was still plenty left for cooking, and this was one delicious recipe that we discovered. Apricots are a delicious alternative to the plums, if you prefer.

Serves 6–8

Pastry

100 g (4 oz) plain flour
50 g (2 oz) butter
25 g (1 oz) caster sugar
1 egg, lightly beaten

Filling

100 g (4 oz) butter, softened
100 g (4 oz) caster sugar
2 eggs and 1 egg yolk
25 g (1 oz) ground almonds
2.5 ml (½ tsp) almond essence
100 g (4 oz) self raising flour
30 ml (2 tbsp) lemon juice
30 ml (2 tbsp) milk
225 g (8 oz) plums, halved and stoned
60 ml (4 tbsp) plum jam
25 g (1 oz) flaked almonds

1. To make the pastry, sieve the flour into a bowl and rub in the butter until the mixture resembles fine breadcrumbs. Stir in the sugar.

2. Mix in the egg with a knife, then knead together lightly to form a smooth pastry. Chill in the refrigerator for ½ hour.

3. Turn onto a floured surface and roll out. Use to line a 20 cm (8 in) deep flan dish. Prick the base, then chill for a short time. Bake blind in a preheated oven at 200°C, LOW power microwave for 5 minutes.

4. Cream together the butter and sugar then beat in the eggs. Fold in the almonds, essence, flour, lemon juice and milk.

5. Arrange the plums in the base of the flan and spread over the jam, if necessary warming this a little in the microwave first.

6. Spoon over the cake mixture and smooth over the top. Sprinkle over the almonds and bake in a preheated oven at 200°C, LOW power microwave for 15–20 minutes or until well risen and golden brown.

OLD ENGLISH SYRUP TART

Nearly everyone likes syrup tart. This one is a little different with the addition of grated apple which takes the edge off the sweetness and is a good old standby.

Serves 6–8

Pastry

200 g (8 oz) plain flour
50 g (2 oz) margarine
50 g (2 oz) lard
45 ml (3 tbsp) cold water

Filling

450 g (1 lb) golden syrup
50 g (2 oz) breadcrumbs
2.5 ml (½ tsp) ginger
grated rind and juice of 1 lemon
15 ml (1 tbsp) cream
1 eating apple, peeled, cored and grated

1. Rub the fat into the flour, add the water and knead gently until smooth. Use ⅔ to line a 20 cm (8 in) flan dish. Keep the trimmings.

2. Warm the syrup on HIGH power microwave for 1 minute. Add all the other ingredients and stir well to mix. Pour the filling into the flan.

3. Roll the pastry trimmings out, cut into strips and use to make a lattice pattern over the filling.

4. Bake in a preheated oven at 200°C, LOW power microwave for 20 minutes. Serve when cold.

BAKEWELL TART

The dictionary describes this as 'a tart containing an almond flavoured pudding mixture over a layer of jam and a town in Derbyshire'. The description is exactly right and the place it was first made must have been Bakewell. Lucky people they were on to a winner, this is delicious.

Serves 6

Pastry

150 g (6 oz) plain flour

40 g (1½ oz) margarine

40 g (1½ oz) lard

30 ml (2 tbsp) cold water

Filling

15 ml (1 tbsp) raspberry jam

50 g (2 oz) butter

50 g (2 oz) caster sugar

1 egg

rind and juice of ½ lemon

50 g (2 oz) ground almonds

50 g (2 oz) cake crumbs

30 ml (2 oz) milk

Icing

150 g (6 oz) icing sugar

15 ml (1 tbsp) hot water

4 glace cherries, halved (optional)

angelica (optional)

1. Rub the fat into the flour and mix to a pastry with the water.

2. Roll out the pastry and line a 20 cm (8 in) flan dish. Spread the pastry base with the jam.

3. Cream the butter and sugar until light and fluffy (soften the butter in the microwave if necessary).

4. Gradually beat in the egg and stir in the lemon and the rest of the ingredients.

5. Bake in a preheated oven at 200°C, LOW power microwave for 20 minutes; it should feel firm.

6. When cool cover with glace icing made by mixing the icing sugar and water together and decorate with glace cherries and angelica leaves, if desired.

See photograph page 101

ORANGE CREAM FLAN

A delicious orange custard dessert topped with fresh oranges. The filling is like a baked orange custard and can be used to make an orange 'creme caramel'.

Serves 6–8

Pastry

100 g (4 oz) plain flour

50 g (2 oz) butter

25 g (1 oz) caster sugar

1 egg, lightly beaten

Filling

300 ml (½ pt) orange juice, fresh or unsweetened

2 oranges

3 egg whites

40 g (1½ oz) caster sugar

1. To make the pastry, sieve the flour into a bowl and rub in the fat until the mixture resembles fine breadcrumbs. Stir in the sugar.

2. Mix in the egg with a knife, then knead together lightly to form a smooth pastry. Chill in the refrigerator for ½ hour.

3. Turn onto a floured surface and roll out. Use to line a 20 cm (8 in) flan dish. Prick the base, then chill for a short time.

4. Heat the orange juice on HIGH power in the microwave for 3 minutes, then beat in the grated rind of 1 orange, the eggs and sugar.

5. Pour into the flan and bake in a preheated oven at 180°C, LOW power microwave for 20 minutes or until the filling is set.

6. Cool the flan then peel and slice the oranges and use to decorate the top.

GRAPE AND MINCEMEAT LATTICE TART

This is an easy very pretty flan that will have the complements pouring in. It is too good to keep just for Christmas so make it whenever seedless grapes are available. The almond pastry could be used for other flans when a sweet pastry is required.

Serves 6

Almond pastry

225 g (8 oz) plain flour

125 g (4 oz) butter

25 g (1 oz) flaked almonds

15 g (½ oz) caster sugar

1 egg yolk

100 ml (4 tbsp) water

Filling

350 g (12 oz) good quality mincemeat

175 g (6 oz) seedless green grapes, halved

25 g (1 oz) flaked almonds

Decoration

6 glace cherries

12 whole blanched almonds

1 egg white

15 ml (1 level tbsp) demerara sugar

1. Rub the fat into the flour until it resembles breadcrumbs, then add the slightly crushed flaked almonds.

2. Mix the sugar, egg yolk and water together and add to the flour. Mix and knead lightly until smooth.

3. Roll out the pastry and use to line a 20 cm (8 in) flan dish. Keep the trimmings.

4. Mix all the filling ingredients together and spoon into the flan.

5. Roll out the trimmings and cut in strips 1.2 cm (½ in) wide, twist the strips and arrange in a lattice pattern over the flan.

6. Place the halved cherries and almonds in alternate squares. Brush the pastry with the lightly beaten egg whites and sprinkle with demerara sugar.

7. Bake at 190°C, LOW power microwave for 20 minutes. Serve whilst still warm.

See cover photograph

BAKED CHEESE CAKE

This is a moist cake, similar in texture to the Jewish type of cheese cake. It is not too sweet and is less rich than the set chilled cheese cake. No other topping than a sprinkling of icing sugar is required.

Serves 8

75 g (3 oz) butter

175 g (6 oz) digestive biscuits, crushed

5 ml (1 level tsp) cinnamon

175 g (6 oz) cream cheese

175 g (6 oz) cottage cheese

75 g (3 oz) caster sugar

25 g (1 oz) cornflour

grated rind and juice of 1 lemon

150 ml (¼ pt) soured cream

2 eggs, separated

50 g (2 oz) sultanas

To serve

icing sugar

1. Melt the butter in the microwave on HIGH power for 2 minutes. Stir in the digestive biscuits and cinnamon.

2. Grease and line the base of a 20 cm (8 in) deep cake dish. Press the digestive biscuits into the base.

3. Put the cream cheese and cottage cheese into a liquidizer or food processor. Mix together the sugar and cornflour and add to the liquidizer along with the lemon rind and juice, soured cream and egg yolks. Blend until smooth.

4. Whisk the egg whites until stiff, then add the cheese mixture and sultanas and fold together. Pour on top of the digestive biscuit base.

5. Bake in a preheated oven at 190°C, HIGH power microwave for 5 minutes, then LOW power for 12 minutes.

6. Leave to cool before turning out and serving, dusted with icing sugar.

See photograph page 104

TARTE AUX POIRES

A classic French recipe, but not that difficult to do. When pears are in season it is a lovely dessert to make, looks beautiful and tastes even better. It is best served the same day it is made. A couple of hints that will help are: firstly, do not be tempted to leave the peeled pears in cold water, use them immediately (the wetness dilutes the custard). Secondly, brush the completed tart with the glaze as soon as it is cool.

Serves 8

Pate sucree

110 g (4 oz) butter, softened

110 g (4 oz) caster sugar (vanilla sugar is best)

4 egg yolks

2.5 ml (½ tsp) vanilla essence (omit if vanilla sugar is used)

225 g (8 oz) plain flour

Filling

125 ml (¼ pt) double cream

2 eggs

25 g (1 oz) caster sugar

2.5 ml (½ tsp) vanilla essence

4 ripe pears, round flat shape are best eg: comice

Glaze

90 ml (6 tbsp) apricot jam

15 ml (1 tbsp) lemon juice

1. Mix all the pastry ingredients, except the flour, in a mixer or with a wooden spoon until just mixed. Add the flour and knead until smooth. Chill for at least an hour.

2. Roll out and use to line a 23–25 cm (9–10 in) metal flan dish. Chill or freeze for an hour.

3. Mix all the filling ingredients together except the pears.

4. Peel the pears, slice in half long ways and core carefully. Place each half flat side down and slice across to form narrow slices.

5. Carefully lift into the flan and arrange 7 halves with the pointed end inwards. Round off the last one and put in the centre.

6. Pour round the filling mixture and put in the preheated oven. Bake for 16 minutes at 190°C, LOW power microwave, check to see if the filling is set by inserting a skewer in the centre. It should come out clean; if not cook a couple of minutes more.

7. Remove the tart and cool. Gently heat the jam and lemon juice in the microwave; sieve.

8. Brush the hot apricot glaze gently onto the tart starting in the centre. Do not go back over areas you have already started.

See photograph page 104

CHEATS APPLE STRUDEL

This strudel is guaranteed to impress and is quicker to make than an apple pie. Best served hot and in fact it can be cooked in your combination oven while you are eating the main course.

Serves 6

1 small packet puff pastry
30 ml (2 tbsp) jam
6 digestive biscuits, crushed
5 ml (1 level tsp) cinnamon
50 g (2 oz) sultanas
450 g (1 lb) cooking apples grated, or thinly sliced

1. Roll out the pastry as large as possible, at least 50 cm (18 in) square. Spread with the jam. Sprinkle on the digestives, cinnamon and sultanas.

2. Cover with the apple leaving 2.5 cm (1 in) around the edge.

3. Roll up neatly and place the join underneath on a baking tray. Bake at 200°C, LOW power microwave for 16 minutes or until golden.

4. Dust well with icing sugar and serve.

———— **VARIATION** ————
Brush the rolled out pastry with 50 g (2 oz) melted butter instead of the jam and sprinkle with a little sugar. This would make a traditional strudel.

RHUBARB AND GINGER CRUMBLE

A delicious variation of a traditional crumble. It is tasty, quick and easy to do. Some delicatessens sell cooking crystalized ginger which is a much cheaper alternative to the crystalized ginger sold in sweet shops.

Serves 4–6

675 g (1½ lb) rhubarb
rind and juice of 1 orange
50 g (2 oz) crystalized ginger, chopped
125 g (4 oz) demerara sugar

Topping

175 g (6 oz) plain flour
125 g (4 oz) soft margarine
150 g (2 oz) rolled oats
75 g (3 oz) demerara sugar
5 ml (1 level tsp) ground ginger

1. Wash and trim the rhubarb and cut into 2.5 cm (1 in) lengths; place in the bottom of a deep 20 cm (8 in) dish.

2. Add the rind and juice of the orange, the chopped ginger and the demerara sugar. Mix.

3. Mix the flour and margarine together until it resembles breadcrumbs, add the oats, ginger and 50 g (2 oz) of the demerara sugar. Stir until mixed, pour over the rhubarb.

4. Sprinkle the remaining demerara over the top and bake in a preheated oven at 200°C, LOW power microwave for 20 minutes or until golden brown.

BLACKBERRY CRUMBLE CAKE

This is really a dessert, but one for sophisticated tastes because it has some very interesting spicy flavours. Prepare the apples the day before to allow the flavours to develop and if you like, prepare the pastry and crumble topping so it only has to be assembled on the day. Serve warm not cold with cream.

Serves 6–8

700 g (1½ lb) Cox's apples, peeled, cored and cut into quarters

75 g (3 oz) brown sugar

2.5 ml (½ tsp) cinnamon

5 ml (1 level tsp) fresh ginger, grated

30 ml (2 tbsp) water

Pastry base

175 g (6 oz) plain flour

75 g (3 oz) butter

75 g (3 oz) caster sugar

1 egg yolk plus 45 ml (3 tbsp) water

Crumble topping

175 g (6 oz) plain flour

5 ml (1 level tsp) ground ginger

5 ml (1 level tsp) cinnamon

2.5 ml (½ tsp) ground coriander

125 g (4 oz) butter

75 g (3 oz) demerara sugar

175 g (6 oz) blackberries, fresh or frozen

1. Mix the first 4 ingredients, add water and microwave, covered on HIGH for 4 minutes, then LOW for 6 minutes. The apples should still keep their shape. Stir, cool and leave overnight.

2. Make the pastry base by rubbing the butter into the flour, add the sugar, the water and egg yolk. Mix well and knead gently. Roll out to line a 20 cm (8 in) pie dish. Chill.

3. To make the topping mix the flour, ginger, cinnamon and coriander together, rub in the butter and stir in the sugar.

4. Put the pastry base into a preheated oven at 200°C, LOW power microwave for 5 minutes, then pile the apples onto the pastry base.

5. Sprinkle on the blackberries and cover with the crumble topping. Bake in the preheated oven at 200°C, LOW power microwave for 20 minutes.

FRUIT CRUMBLE

There is nothing better in the winter than a good old fashioned crumble, especially when it can be cooked with such speed. Use any seasonal fruit and perk up the flavour by adding a little cinnamon or other spice to the fruit or crumble topping.

Serves 4–6

675 g (1½ lb) peeled and cored or stoned fruit, eg. apples, plums etc

sugar

150 g (6 oz) plain flour

75 g (3 oz) butter

50 g (2 oz) caster sugar

1. Place the fruit in a 1.5 lit (2½ pt) souffle dish and sprinkle with sugar to taste.

2. Sieve the flour into a bowl then rub in the butter until the mixture resembles fine breadcrumbs. Stir in the sugar.

3. Spoon the mixture over the fruit and bake in a preheated oven at 200°C, LOW power microwave for 20 minutes. Serve hot with custard.

—— **VARIATION** ——
Use 150 g (6 oz) muesli mixed with 75 g (3 oz) melted butter and a little brown sugar as an alternative topping.

LINZER TORTE

A traditional continental cake. There are many variations on the recipe, and this is one of the best. It is a rich spicy almond pastry filled with sweetened raspberries and decorated with a lattice of pastry then glazed with redcurrant jelly which looks absolutely beautiful and is served cold as a dessert or a tea time cake.

Serves 8

Pastry

100 g (4 oz) butter
225 g (8 oz) plain flour
100 g (4 oz) caster sugar
50 g (2 oz) ground unblanched almonds
2.5 ml (½ level tsp) cinnamon
grated rind of ½ a lemon
1 whole egg and a yolk

Filling

300 g (1¼ lb) raspberries
50 g (2 oz) sugar
50 g (2 oz) redcurrant jelly

1. Soften the butter in the microwave, HIGH power for 1 minute. It should be spreadable.

2. In a mixer, put the flour, sugar, almonds, cinnamon and lemon rind. Add the soft butter and egg, mix together well.

3. Wrap the pastry in cling film and cool for an hour.

4. Sweeten the raspberries with the sugar. If they are fresh, microwave on HIGH for 3 minutes to soften. If the raspberries are frozen it is not necessary.

5. Roll the pastry out, to line a 20 cm (8 in) flan dish. Keep the trimmings.

6. Fill the flan with raspberries and arrange a lattice of pastry trimmings on the top.

7. Bake in a preheated oven at 200°C, LOW power microwave for 20 minutes.

8. When the flan is cool melt the redcurrant jelly for 1 minute on HIGH power microwave and brush over the flan.

See photograph page 103

RASPBERRY GATEAU

Gateaux are usually very rich and should never ordinarily be chosen at the end of a heavy meal. This one is the exception! It is so light that it melts in the mouth and as there is so little sugar in it, the flavour is sharp and refreshing.

Serves 6–8

40 g (1½ oz) butter
3 eggs
75 g (3 oz) caster sugar
65 g (2½ oz) plain flour
15 ml (1 level tbsp) cornflour

To finish

300 ml (½ pt) double cream
350 g (12 oz) raspberries, fresh or frozen

1. Grease and line the base of a 20 cm (8 in) cake dish with grease-proof paper. Melt the butter in the microwave on HIGH for 1–1½ minutes. Set aside to cool.

2. Place the eggs and sugar in a large bowl and whisk over a pan of hot water until pale and thick. The mixture should leave a trail when the whisk is lifted.

3. Remove the bowl from the pan and whisk for a few minutes until cool.

4. Sift together the flour and cornflour, then fold half of it into the egg mixture. Trickle the butter in, down the side of the bowl, then fold in with the remaining flour.

5. Turn the mixture into the cake dish and bake in a preheated oven at 225°C, LOW power microwave for 10–12 minutes or until golden, and a skewer inserted into the middle comes out clean.

6. Leave for 5 minutes in the cake dish before turning out onto a wire rack to cool.

7. Whip the cream until thick. Cut the cake in half and spread half the cream in the middle. Cover with raspberries, reserving a few to decorate the top.

8. Replace the top of the cake and spread the remaining cream on top, piping rosettes around the edge if desired. Decorate with raspberries and serve.

WALNUT AND COFFEE GATEAU WITH STRAWBERRIES

A really luscious cake for those times when you want something dramatic for a dessert. Easy to make if you have an electric mixer, otherwise it requires a good strong arm!

Serves 8

4 eggs
150 g (5 oz) caster sugar
125 g (4 oz) plain flour
50 g (2 oz) walnuts, coarsely chopped
30 ml (2 tbsp) coffee essence (camp coffee)

Filling

450 g (1 lb) strawberries
600 ml (1 pt) double or whipping cream
15 ml (1 tbsp) caster sugar

1. Whisk the eggs and sugar over hot water as you would for a whisked sponge or whisk with an electric mixer until thick and leaving a trail.

2. Fold in the flour, walnuts and coffee essence. Turn into a 20 cm (8 in) cake dish that has been greased, base lined and dusted with caster sugar and flour.

3. Bake in a preheated oven at 190°C, LOW power microwave for 16–20 minutes until firm. Turn out to cool.

4. Slice the strawberries reserving a few for decoration. Whip the cream until lightly whipped. Combine ⅔ of the cream with the strawberries and sugar.

5. Split the cake into three layers and sandwich with the strawberry cream.

6. Spread the remaining cream over the top and decorate with strawberries.

See photograph page 103

CHOCOLATE SOUFFLE

This is wonderful for a light dessert, so impressive and really quite easy to make with a combination oven. Make the sauce and cover with a circle of grease-proof paper. Have the egg white ready to beat and then 10 minutes before you plan to serve the souffle you can finish it off. Serve with lashings of single cream.

Serves 6

300 ml (½ pt) milk
75 g (3 oz) butter
50 g (2 oz) flour
50 g (2 oz) caster sugar
100 g (4 oz) plain chocolate, grated
4 eggs, separated

1. Put the milk, butter and flour into a large bowl or jug and microwave on HIGH for 2 minutes.

2. Whisk well and microwave for another 2 minutes, on HIGH, whisking again at the end of the cooking time. The sauce should be thick and smooth.

3. Add the chocolate, stir and microwave for another minute on HIGH. Stir again, then cool.

4. Turn the oven to preheat to 200°C.

5. Add the egg yolks and sugar to the sauce, then whisk the egg whites until stiff and fold in the sauce mixture.

6. Turn into a greased 1.5 lit (2½ pt) souffle dish. Bake in a preheated oven at 200°C, HIGH power microwave for 8–10 minutes. Dust with icing sugar.

HOT BANANA SOUFFLE

If you like bananas you will love this recipe. It tastes just like really light bananas and although it is delicious on its own, as its colour is pinky brown because of the bananas, it is nicest dusted with icing sugar and served with lots of single cream.

Serves 6

65 g (2½ oz) sugar

15 ml (1 level tbsp) cornflour

a little freshly grated nutmeg

grated rind of ½ lemon

175 ml (6 fl oz) milk

50 g (2 oz) butter

5 ml (1 tsp) vanilla essence

3 medium bananas

juice of ½ lemon

1. Mix the sugar, cornflour, nutmeg and rind together in a jug. Add a little milk and stir until smooth.

2. Add the remaining milk and heat on HIGH power for 2 minutes, or until thick, stirring once.

3. Add the butter and when cooled a little, the egg yolks and vanilla.

4. Mash the bananas with the lemon juice or liquidize until smooth.

5. Whisk the egg whites until stiff then fold with the banana into the sauce mixture until evenly mixed.

6. Turn the mixture into a greased and sugared 1.5 lit (2½ pt) souffle dish and bake in a hot oven at 220°C, HIGH power microwave for 8–10 minutes.

7. Dust with icing sugar and serve immediately.

QUEEN OF PUDDINGS

This pudding really lives up to its name! Using cake crumbs instead of the traditional breadcrumbs makes it more special and the use of the combination oven means that it can be cooked without a bain marie. Try the pudding hot or cold – either way it is equally delicious.

Serves 6

600 ml (1 pt) milk

50 g (2 oz) butter

3 eggs, separated

grated rind of 1 lemon

150 g (5 oz) caster sugar

150 g (5 oz) crumbled trifle sponges, or cake crumbs

60 ml (4 tbsp) jam

To decorate

glace cherries and angelica leaves

1. Heat the milk and butter in a bowl on HIGH power for 4 minutes.

2. Beat the egg yolks, lemon rind and 50 g (2 oz) of caster sugar into the milk.

3. Place the sponge crumbs in a souffle dish and pour over the milk mixture. Bake at 125°C, LOW power microwave for 20 minutes.

4. Remove from the oven. Soften the jam on HIGH power in the microwave for 30 seconds, then spread over the pudding.

5. Whisk the egg whites until stiff then fold in the remaining sugar. Spoon over the pudding and return to the oven at 150°C for a further 10–15 minutes, or until the meringue is crisp and lightly browned. Serve immediately.

––––––– COOK'S TIP –––––––

To make the pudding even more special, use a mixture of sherry and milk to pour over the crumbs or a favourite liqueur jam to spread on the top.

See photograph page 102

BREAD AND BUTTER PUDDING

This is a very old fashioned pudding often badly made, but when properly done it is delicious. The combination oven helps to make it quickly and prevent the custard from curdling. If you have not eaten this since you were at school, try again.

Serves 4

6 thin slices of bread

75 g (3 oz) soft butter

75 g (3 oz) sultanas

3 small eggs or 2 large ones

75 g (3 oz) vanilla sugar or 75 g (3 oz) sugar plus 5 ml (1 tsp) vanilla essence

300 ml (½ pt) milk (creamy or ½ milk ½ cream)

8 almonds, cut into slivers

1. Cut the crusts off the bread and divide into quarters diagonally.

2. Butter the bread generously and also butter a 1.2 lit (2 pt) dish.

3. Layer the bread and sultanas in the dish ending with bread.

4. Beat the eggs and sugar together, add the milk and pour over the bread. Leave to soak for approximately 10 minutes. Sprinkle with the nuts.

5. Bake the bread and butter pudding in a preheated oven 200°C, LOW power microwave for 20 minutes.

EVE'S PUDDING

Eve's pudding always makes one think of Religious Knowledge lessons at school and the stealing of the 'forbidden fruit'! This dessert would certainly tempt anyone and the only feelings of guilt would be for the extra calories eaten! Well worth it! Serve with lashings of custard and forget the calories.

Serves 4

675 g (1½ lb) cooking apples, plums, pears or other fruit

sugar

50 g (2 oz) margarine

50 g (2 oz) caster sugar

1 egg

50 g (2 oz) self raising flour

15 ml (1 tbsp) milk

1. Peel, core and slice the apples or pears, or halve and stone the plums. Place in a 1.5 lit (2½ pt) souffle dish and sprinkle with sugar to taste.

2. Place the margarine, caster sugar, egg and flour in a bowl and beat until smooth and creamy. Beat in the milk.

3. Spread the cake mixture over the fruit and bake in a preheated oven at 200°C, LOW power microwave for 15 minutes. Serve hot with custard or cream.

—— SERVING SUGGESTION ——
The above recipe makes quite a thin layer of sponge over the fruit. For a more substantial pudding use 100 g (4 oz) of margarine, sugar and flour and 2 eggs. Bake for a little longer.

See photograph page 102

LEMON SAUCE PUDDING

This is one of those magical puddings which separate into a layer of very light sponge and a layer of sharp lemon sauce. In a normal oven it needs to be cooked in a bain marie (water bath) but in a combination oven this is not necessary. Just as well because the water always seemed to get spilt all over the kitchen. Try to make this in a straight-sided glass dish – a souffle dish is ideal so that the layers can be appreciated.

Serves 6

50 g (2 oz) butter or soft margarine
200 g (8 oz) caster sugar
4 eggs, separated
grated rind and juice of 2 lemons
50 g (2 oz) self raising flour
250 ml (8 fl oz) milk

1. Cream the butter and sugar together until light and fluffy; a mixer is ideal.

2. Add the egg yolks, rind and juice.

3. Add the flour and gradually add the milk and beat well until smooth.

4. Whisk the egg whites, until stiff and cut into the batter mixture with a metal spoon.

5. Pour the mixture into a greased 1.25 lit (2½ pt) oven-proof dish and bake in a preheated oven at 180°C, LOW power microwave for 20 minutes or until golden on top.

6. Serve hot or cold.

Useful Charts

The following charts are an at-a-glance guide to cooking ingredients in the oven using either your microwave or microwave/combination facility.

MICROWAVING PASTA AND RICE

PASTA/RICE	QUANTITY	PREPARATION	COOKING TIME ON HIGH POWER	TIPS
AMERICAN LONG GRAIN OR PATNA RICE	225 g (8 oz)	Place in deep covered dish with knob of butter. Cover with 600 ml (1 pt) boiling water, salted	12–14 mins. Stand for 5 mins	Stir halfway
BROWN RICE	100 g (4 oz)	600 ml (1 pt) boiling water, salted	30 mins	Stir halfway, drain
MACARONI AND SMALL PASTA NOODLES	225 g (8 oz)	Place in deep dish with 15 ml (1 tbsp) oil and cover with 750 ml (1¼ pt) boiling salted water	8 mins. Stand for 3 mins	Cook uncovered. Stir halfway
SPAGHETTI	225 g (8 oz)	Break in half and place in a dish. Cover with 750 ml (1¼ pt) boiling salted water	10 mins. Stand for 2 mins	Cook uncovered. Stir halfway
LASAGNE	225 g (8 oz)	Add 1 litre (1¾ pt) boiling salted water and 15 ml (1 tbsp) oil	10 mins. Stand for 2 mins	Cook uncovered. Stir halfway

MICROWAVING FRESH FRUIT

FRUIT	QUANTITY	PREPARATION	COOKING TIME ON HIGH POWER
APPLES, (eg. BRAMLEYS)	450 g (1 lb)	Peel, core and slice. Sprinkle with sugar to taste	6–8 mins
APRICOTS	450 g (1 lb)	Stone, wash, sprinkle with sugar to taste. Stir halfway	6–8 mins
BLACKCURRANTS, REDCURRANTS, LOGANBERRIES, BLACKBERRIES etc	450 g (1 lb)	Top and tail, wash and sprinkle with sugar to taste	3–5 mins
GOOSEBERRIES	450 g (1 lb)	Top and tail, wash and sprinkle with sugar to taste	4–5 mins
PEACHES	4 medium sized	Stone and wash – sprinkle with sugar	4–5 mins
PEARS	450 g (1 lb)	Peel, core and cut in half. Dissolve 50–75 g (2–3 oz) sugar in hot water and pour over pears	6–8 mins
PLUMS, CHERRIES, DAMSONS, GREENGAGES	450 g (1 lb)	Stone and wash. Sprinkle with sugar to taste	4–6 mins
RHUBARB	450 g (1 lb)	Wash, trim and cut into short pieces. Add approx 110 g (4 oz) sugar	7–10 mins

MICROWAVING FRESH VEGETABLES

VEGETABLE	QUANTITY	PREPARATION	SALTED WATER	COOKING TIME ON HIGH POWER
ASPARAGUS	450 g (1 lb)	Trim, leave whole	60 ml (4 tbsp)	6–8 mins
AUBERGINES	450 g (1 lb)	Wash, slice, sprinkle with salt. Leave for 30 mins. Rinse before cooking	30 ml (2 tbsp)	8–10 mins
BROAD BEANS	450 g (1 lb)	Remove them from pods	45 ml (3 tbsp)	6–8 mins
FRENCH BEANS	450 g (1 lb)	Wash and cut	30 ml (2 tbsp)	8–10 mins
RUNNER BEANS	450 g (1 lb)	String and slice	30 ml (2 tbsp)	8–10 mins
BEETROOT	450 g (1 lb)	Peel and slice	30 ml (2 tbsp)	8–10 mins
WHOLE BEET	450 g (1 lb)	Scrub and pierce	30 ml (2 tbsp)	12–14 mins
BROCCOLI	450 g (1 lb)	Trim and cut into spears	30 ml (2 tbsp)	8–12 mins
BRUSSEL SPROUTS	450 g (1 lb)	Trim, remove outer leaves and wash	30 ml (2 tbsp)	8–10 mins
CABBAGE	450 g (1 lb)	Wash and shred leaves	30 ml (2 tbsp)	8–10 mins
CARROTS	450 g (1 lb)	New/small: wash, scrape, leave whole. Old: scrape and slice thinly	30 ml (2 tbsp) 30 ml (2 tbsp)	7–10 mins 7–10 mins
CAULIFLOWER	450 g (1 lb)	Cut into florets	60 ml (4 tbsp)	10–12 mins
CELERY	450 g (1 lb)	Wash, trim slice	45 ml (3 tbsp)	7–10 mins
CORN ON THE COB	2 medium	Wrap each in grease-proof paper with knob of butter	—	6–8 mins
COURGETTES	450 g (1 lb)	Wash, trim and slice, add 25 g (1 oz) butter and cover	—	8–10 mins
LEEKS	450 g (1 lb)	Wash, trim and slice	30 ml (2 tbsp)	7–10 mins
MARROW	450 g (1 lb)	Peel, cut into ring 2 cm (¾ in) thick. Remove seeds and ¼ rings	30 ml (2 tbsp)	8–10 mins
ONIONS	2 large	1. Peel and slice 2. Peel and chop	30 ml (2 tbsp) 30 ml (2 tbsp)	6–7 mins 4–5 mins
PARSNIPS	450 g (1 lb)	Peel and slice	30 ml (2 tbsp)	8–10 mins
PEAS	450 g (1 lb)	Remove from pods	30 ml (2 tbsp)	8–10 mins
POTATOES: NEW	450 g (1 lb)	Wash thoroughly but leave in skin	90 ml (6 tbsp)	6–8 mins
POTATOES: OLD	450 g (1 lb)	Wash and scrub thoroughly, dry and prick with a fork	—	8–10 mins
SPINACH	450 g (1 lb)	Wash, break up thick stalks	—	6–8 mins
SPRING GREENS	450 g (1 lb)	Wash, break up thick stalks and shred	30 ml (2 tbsp)	6–8 mins
SWEDE	450 g (1 lb)	Peel and dice	30 ml (2 tbsp)	7–8 mins
WHOLE SWEDE	450 g (1 lb)	Scrub and cut a slice from the base, turn halfway, stand 5 mins at end	300 ml (½ pt) hot	12–14 mins
TOMATOES	450 g (1 lb)	Wash and halve Cover	—	3–6 mins
TURNIPS	450 g (1 lb)	Peel and slice	30 ml (2 tbsp)	8–10 mins
WHOLE TURNIP	450 g (1 lb)	Scrub and cut a slice from the bottom, turn halfway, leave to stand 5 mins	300 ml (½ pt) hot	10–12 mins

DEFROSTING AND MICROWAVING FISH

FISH	QUANTITY	DEFROSTING TIME AT LOW POWER	COOKING TIME AT HIGH POWER
WHITE FISH – COD, HADDOCK, COLEY, PLAICE OR SOLE	450 g (1 lb) prepared fillets	5 mins. Stand for 5 mins	4–6 mins
HERRING, TROUT AND MACKEREL	225 g (8 oz) fish gutted but whole	5 mins. Stand for 10–15 mins	4–6 mins
KIPPERS	450 g (1 lb) fillets	5 mins. Stand for 5–10 mins	3–5 mins
SMOKED FISH, HADDOCK OR COD	450 g (1 lb)	5 mins. Stand for 5 mins	4–5 mins
SALMON STEAKS	450 g (1 lb)	5 mins. Stand for 5 mins	4–5 mins
SHELL FISH: PRAWNS, SCAMPI	450 g (1 lb)	2 mins. Stand for 10 mins	Use as required

COOKING MEAT OR POULTRY

MEAT OR POULTRY	TEMPERATURE	POWER LEVEL	TIME PER 450 g (1 lb)	TIPS
BEEF: RARE	220°C	Low	10 mins	
MEDIUM	200°C	Low	13 mins	
WELL DONE	180°C	Low	16 mins	
LAMB: MEDIUM	200°C	Low	18–20 mins	Leave to stand for 10–15 mins before covering
WELL DONE	200°C	Low	20–22 mins	
PORK	200°C	Low	20–22 mins	
GAMMON	See recipe			
CHICKEN	200°C	Low	12–15 mins	
DUCK	220°C	Medium	8–10 mins	
TURKEY	220°C	Low	8 mins	Turn halfway, leave for 10 mins then the juices should run clear
PHEASANT	See recipe			
PIGEON	See recipe			
OTHER GAME BIRDS	200°C	Low	9–10 mins	
PORTIONS OF MEAT				
CHICKEN QUARTERS (4)	200°C	Low	16–20 mins	
CHICKEN EIGHTS (4)	200°C	Low	12–15 mins	
LAMB CHOPS (4)	200°C	Low	12–14 mins	
PORK CHOPS (4)	220°C	Low	12–14 mins	

Index

Directions In Art

Louisa Sherman & ...

Heinemann
LIBRARY

First published in Great Britain by Heinemann Library, Halley Court, Jordan Hill, Oxford OX2 8EJ, part of Harcourt Education.
Heinemann is a registered trademark of Harcourt Education Ltd.

Editorial: Lucy Thunder and Helen Cannons
Design: Jo Hinton-Malivoire and AMR
Picture Research: Hannah Taylor and Elaine Willis
Production: Edward Moore

Originated by Ambassador Litho Ltd
Printed and bound in China by South China Printing Company

ISBN 0 431 17645 0 (hardback)
07 06 05 04 03
10 9 8 7 6 5 4 3 2 1

ISBN 0 431 17655 8 (paperback)
08 07 06 05 04
10 9 8 7 6 5 4 3 2 1

British Library Cataloguing in Publication Data
Sherman, Louisa and Hofmeyr, Dianne
Printmaking. – (Directions in art)
769.9
A full catalogue record for this book is available from the British Library.

Acknowledgements
The Publishers would like to thank the following for permission to reproduce photographs: Art Resource / The Andy Warhol Foundation for the Visual Arts / ARS, NY and DACS p. **41**; Vija Celmins / McKee Gallery pp. **13**, **14**; Corbis / George H Huey p. **4**; Alan Cristea Gallery / Richard Hamilton 2003. All rights reserved, DACS p. **21**; Peter Diog / Tate London 2003 pp. **17**, **18**; Durst p. **34**; William Kentridge pp. **25**, **27**; David Krut Fine Art Inc. p. **26**; The Estate of Roy Lichtenstein / DACS 2003 pp. **29t**, **30**; Andrew Mummery Gallery pp. **9**, **11**; National Gallery of Art, Washington p. **15**; Niedersachsische Landesmuseum, Hanover, Germany / Bridgeman Art Library / The Andy Warhol Foundation for the Visual Arts / ARS, NY and DACS 2003 p. **42**; Julian Opie / Alan Cristea Gallery pp. **33**, **35**; Paula Rego / Courtesy of Marlborough Fine Art, London pp. **37**, **39**; Tate London 2003 / Richard Hamilton 2003. All Rights Reserved, DACS p. **23**; Kim Westcott p. **45**; Adrian Wiszniewski / Glasgow Print Studio p. **47**, / The Paragon Press pp. **48**, **49**.

Cover photograph of *Portrait of Dieter Roth* (1998) by Richard Hamilton reproduced with permission of Alan Cristea Gallery / Richard Hamilton 2003. All rights reserved DACS.

The publishers would like to thank Richard Stemp, Gallery Educator at the Tate, London, for his assistance in the preparation of this book

CONTENTS

Any words appearing in the text in bold, **like this**, are explained in the Glossary.

WHAT IS PRINTMAKING?

We can all remember the pleasure of making footprints in the sand or drawing in soil with a stick. These kinds of basic images were also made by early cave dwellers whose handprints on rock faces were the first, direct prints. Since early times handprints were made as either positive or negative images. Positive prints were the most common and the hand was covered in paint and then printed directly on to the rock face. Positive handprints, as you can see in the picture below, were made by using the hand as a stencil and spraying around it with paint. The same imagination behind those first prints prompted a rich tradition of prints and printmaking that followed down the centuries.

Today, we think of a print as a work of art printed in ink on paper of which there are multiple copies. Prints are art works created not by drawing directly on to paper, but by an indirect method. The image is made on to a surface such as wood, metal or stone and then transferred to paper. In this way, multiple copies of the work can be made.

These handprints, from the famous Painted Cave at the Anasazi ruins in Arizona, USA, are an early example of printmaking. They were made around AD 450 to AD 1300.

Traditional methods of printmaking

In traditional printmaking, artists work directly on to their chosen surface to produce an image, often with the help of master printers who are trained specifically to produce prints. There are several different ways to do this. Artists using **relief printing** techniques such as **woodcut** or wood engraving will cut an image directly into the woodblock.

In **intaglio** techniques, such as drypoint (see pages 26–27), **etching** (see page 38) and aquatint (see page 18), artists press ink into lines etched or engraved into the surface of a **plate**. In **lithography**, the artist draws directly with a greasy crayon on to a flat limestone slab before it is treated for printing. In **screenprint** artists prepare their own stencils for printing. These methods were commonly used in the 19th and early 20th centuries, but later new technologies such as photography and **digital printing** have brought about far-reaching changes in printmaking.

Lithography

Lithography is a printmaking technique in which the image is drawn on to a flat slab of limestone or a specially prepared metal plate. Drawings can be made with greasy pencils, crayons or lithographic ink, also called *tusche*. The plate or stone is then treated to retain water in the areas not drawn on. When the stone or plate is rolled up with printing ink, the greasy drawing picks up the ink. The rest of the stone or plate retains water and will repel ink. A sheet of paper is placed on to the inked plate or stone and is then passed through a lithographic press. The image transfers from the stone or metal surface, to the paper.

Picasso's Le Picador II *(1961) is a lithographic print.*

20th century prints and photography

Not only do the best artists of our time make prints, some of the best artworks of our time are prints. SALLY TALLMAN, 1996

Important artists like Pablo Picasso (1881–1973), Henri Matisse (1869–1954) and Emile Nolde (1867–1956) turned increasingly to printmaking in the 20th century. Gradually, printmaking became a major form of artistic expression, taking its place alongside painting, drawing and sculpture.

Fine art printmaking also thrived as a result of the invention of photography in 1839. Before then, printmaking had been used to produce all kinds of everyday material, such as advertisements. Photography meant that mechanical printing processes were increasingly used to produce such work, freeing printmaking by hand to develop as an art form in its own right. Photography also played an important role in printmaking in other respects. Photographs became a source for images within printmaking, and photographic techniques were used to transfer images from film to screen or plate.

Many artists including Richard Hamilton (pages 20–23) and Andy Warhol (pages 40–43) produced some of their most significant works of art on paper using photographic techniques. The use of photography in printmaking caused a stir. It was thought by some to undermine the idea of the 'original' print.

The 'original' print

In traditional printmaking, the artist is directly involved in the creation of the print. Artists and printers aim to produce prints that are identical and they number the **editions**. If **print-runs** are too big, there is the danger of losing print quality. Also, too many copies of a print could reduce its value. It is therefore in the interests of artist and art dealers to control the production of 'original prints'. However, over recent years the idea of the 'original' print has been challenged by new ideas and technologies. Artists searching for new ways to express themselves have broadened the idea of printmaking beyond just handmade images. Another breakthrough that challenged what is considered 'original' was the first computer-generated prints made in London in the 1960s.

A new freedom in printmaking

The recent use of digital printing has, similar to photography before it, created new opportunities and challenges for the printmaking world. Traditionally, a print-run is limited to how long the **plate** or screen will last until it becomes worn and the image deteriorates. However digital printing can result in print-runs of thousands. Furthermore, new inks and papers with increased permanence have been specially developed and compare well with traditional papers and inks.

In digital printing, images may be recorded by camera and loaded on to computers for further manipulation before printing on paper or other materials. Digital printmaking has opened up exciting new possibilities for artists to explore in terms of technique. For example, Hamilton transfers his thorough understanding of photographic printmaking techniques to his digital printmaking, while Chila Kumari Burman (pages 8–11) and Julian Opie (pages 32–35) use digital images in their **installations** to create multiple prints for wallpaper and to compose murals and even car bumper stickers!

While many contemporary artists explore new digital technologies, others, like Kim Westcott (pages 44–45) and William Kentridge (pages 24–27), use old techniques in a new way. Westcott revives a traditional wax painting technique for her printmaking and Kentridge creates etchings, linocuts and **photogravure** prints that could almost be seen as 'stills' from his animated films. Others, such as Warhol and Hamilton, explored **conceptual** art issues in printmaking – where the idea behind the work is all-important. By doing this they brought printmaking, in the 1960s, into line with sculpture and painting. They also took up the French **Dada** and **Surrealist** artist Marcel Duchamp's (1887–1968) earlier idea that art is a 'choice of mind, not the cleverness of hand'. Duchamp exhibited a 'ready made' porcelain urinal entitled *Fountain* (1917), to illustrate that a work of art is determined by the artist's 'choice of mind' rather than the practical skills of painting, sculpture or printmaking.

Although the 'hand' of the artist or master printer still has to ink the plate, or click the computer key, it is exciting to see how printmaking contributes in a significant and varied way to today's art.

CHILA KUMARI BURMAN

Chila Kumari Burman is an artist whose works span printmaking, painting, drawing, mixed **media**, photography, video and film. She was born in 1957 in Liverpool, UK, and grew up near the seaside in Formby. At home the family spoke Punjabi, but Burman attended English schools in Liverpool before doing a Foundation Course at the Southport College of Art. She also attended the Slade School of Fine Art in London where she graduated in Fine Art in Printmaking in 1982. Burman has taught at different art schools across Britain. She has exhibited her work in Britain and in India, Canada, USA, Pakistan, Cuba and Africa. She lives and works in Haringey, London.

Influences from home and beyond

Burman's art reflects her own life very closely, dealing with her identity as an Asian woman. She explores the stereotype of Asian women being 'meek, mild and passive', as well as her own family history. **Dada**, **Surrealism**, Bollywood, Hindu philosophy, film, music, popular culture and her mother have all influenced her. Burman's heartfelt piece *Dad on a ship coming to Britain in the 50's and the three Queens* (1995) features her mother. The work shows three queens – her mother, her grandmother and the portrait of the Queen of England on a banknote. All three women are represented as queens in recognition of their endurance and achievements. By combining these pictures Burman cleverly shows us that she moves between two different cultures – her own Indian background and her life in Britain.

> *My recent work is concerned with autobiography, representation of the self, I have dealt with themes around history, dual cultural heritage, mythology, memory and photography, wild women...*
> CHILA KUMARI BURMAN

Working method

Burman uses a range of media including painting, photography and **digital printmaking** to suit the **installation** or display of her works in exhibition spaces. She often combines different techniques and unusual media such as **laser prints** and car spray paint. She also uses 'found' images and personal photographs that she reworks to explore the themes in her work. For example, in *Hello Girls* (1999) Burman, exhibited rows and rows of prints to form one large work.

Hello Girls is a reflection on the successful 1990s Wonderbra® advertisements, 'Hello Boys', which featured an alluring, 'sexy' image of a woman in a bra. In *Hello Girls*, Burman deals with western stereotypes and the portrayal of the Asian female, including taboos such as bras and breasts in Asian culture. Her work questions the attitudes towards women in these advertisements, in particular Asian and African women.

For-tune

In *For-tune* (2002; **Cibachrome**/Ilfochrome classic print on plastic paper),
Burman further explores the coloured, patterned bras used in *Hello Girls*. Here
she elaborates upon the idea of bras, but adds colourful flowers and *bindis* that
she blends into an exotic, sumptuous array of colours, patterns and textures.

Ideals of beauty

Burman includes elements in *For-tune* such as the *bindi* and flowers that remind us of Hindu temples. The *bindi* is a traditional Hindu decoration applied to the forehead that marks the third eye, the home of conscious and sub-conscious awareness and thought in Hindu culture. Although the *bindi* has become a popular body decoration worldwide, Burman subtly questions whether we understand the significance of the *bindi* in Hindu culture. She does this in a playful and colourful manner, even though her concerns are serious. In *For-tune*, the artist protests against the modern preoccupation with glamour and beauty; she claims freedom for women to do with their bodies what they want and not to become slaves to the fashion industry.

We can look with pleasure at *For-tune's* beautiful colours and shapes, but Burman also reminds us that we should appreciate the female body with thoughtfulness, even the bodies of those we do not know well. She presents the viewer with a Hindu visual ideal of beauty, in contrast to Western ideals of beauty, desire and identity that dominate the **mass media**.

Technique

Burman uses a collage technique in *For-tune* to piece together this bright **composition**. She collected objects including animal prints and brightly coloured bras that represent Western fashion and beauty, and flowers and *bindis* that recall Hindu culture. She then arranged them in eight different compositions on a colour laser printer. After making the colour prints, she worked on the copies and re-photographed the completed eight images that were then printed to make up a larger Cibachrome.

A Cibachrome or C-Print is a high quality photographic printing process on to plastic paper. Images are printed from slides or transparencies on to paper that contains special dyes built into the paper rather than on the surface as in conventional colour prints. The process is known for its stable, fade-resistant brilliance and intense, sharp colours.

Girl art across cultures

In many ways Burman has been a groundbreaking artist in Britain who has become actively involved in issues of identity, class and gender. The 1980s, when Burman started practising her art, was a significant time in the British art world for many African, Asian and Caribbean artists.

There were many debates about race, identity and the role of art. These discussions helped to give a voice and identity to people from varied cultural backgrounds. Burman explores the issues of being a British–Asian. She also incorporates elements of other people's experiences of crossing from one culture into another.

In a work entitled *Automatic Rap: Don't Get Me Started* (1994), Burman explores how identities become merged by combining elements from punk, *bhangra* (Punjab folk music), reggae, rap, hip-hop, Hindi films, pop star imagery, graffiti and her own adolescence. This self-portrait has a rap text written over it: 'Wish I could go to discos, parties, dances, and have girlfriends and boyfriends like all the english girls and posh asian girls … hibernate to liberate – Don't get me started … let's Laugh and Dance … STRUGGLE, FIGHT, SHOUT, IZZAT/ RESPECT US NOW'.

In *Blue Apsaras* (1999), Burman explores the beauty of apsaras who are ancient Vedic Indian water and forest spirits. This work explores the cultural restrictions Asian women face in terms of dress. They are constantly torn between Western and Asian ways of behaviour.

Blue Apsaras *(1999) was created from collaged colour photocopies that were then photographed and printed as Cibachrome prints.*

VIJA CELMINS

Vija Celmins is a well known American painter, object-maker and **draughtswoman**. She is also a skilled printmaker using a wide range of processes in her art including wood **engraving**, **mezzotint** and stone **lithography**.

Celmins was born in Riga, the capital of Latvia, Eastern Europe, in 1938. During her childhood, the Celmins family escaped from war-torn Europe and eventually settled in Indianapolis, USA. Celmins graduated in 1962 with a degree in Fine Arts then moved to Los Angeles where she completed a Masters in Fine Arts from the University of California. She then joined their teaching staff. Celmins has since moved to New York where she lives and works. She has exhibited widely both in the USA and Europe.

Influences

While still at school and before she could speak any English, Celmins used to draw and paint. Some years later she spent a summer at Yale University where she came into contact with a group of artists and students, who influenced her to become a painter. Since the 1960s Celmins has used photographs as inspiration. A single photograph may serve as the basis for several different works of art.

Approach

Celmin's early **still-lives** are painted in an almost monochromatic, or single colour, palette of soft greys and whites. They reveal a sense of sadness and desolation that could be traced to her memories of violence and homelessness during her early childhood. From 1966 her focus shifted away from painting and she concentrated on detailed graphite pencil drawings of the sea, the desert and night skies.

Celmins has a fascination with space. After studying black and white photographs from expeditions to the moon in the 1960s, she realized that the layers of stars in the sky created distance. She believed that putting layers in drawings can prompt the viewer's thought processes and create a depth in the relationship between the viewer and the art object.

Celmin's printmaking extends over more than 35 **editions** made during the last 30 years. Of these, the *Sky*, *Ocean*, *Desert* and *Galaxy* prints are probably the most important as they represent the central themes in her work (see pages 14–15).

Celmins has been interested in the subject of spiders for several years. In *Web #2: Mezzotint* (2000), she portrays the delicate strands of the spider web in her usual grey shades. The mezzotint technique is ideal to achieve the continuous graded tones in this subtle image. The idea of layering also occurs in the spider's web. While looking at the finely drawn detail and observing the whole **composition** with its shifts of light and darkness, the viewer becomes trapped.

Web #2: Mezzotint *(2000). The fragile nature of a spider's web, that is both a nest and a trap, seems a reflection on the artist's traumatic childhood and loss of her home during World War II.*

Mezzotint

Mezzotint is a time-consuming printing process. First a tool with a serrated edge is used to roughen the **plate** all over, creating ridges called burrs. The design is made by polishing the plate smooth in some places and scraping to flatten the burrs in others. Some areas may be left with just the rough burrs exposed. The plate is then covered in ink, which is retained by all the rough parts. This creates a strong black when printed. The smoother parts hold less ink and so print a lighter tone. In this way a range of different tones are used to make up the image. The term mezzotint comes from the Italian *mezzo* meaning half and *tinto* meaning tint.

Ocean Surfaces 2000

Ocean Surfaces 2000 (2000), a wood engraving, is an interpretation of a photograph taken at Venice Beach, California. The finished engraving can easily be mistaken for a photograph as it has been cut in such a precise, realistic and detailed manner. Celmins has captured the movement and play of light upon the water without the images having an end or a beginning. There is no indication of scale. The distance between the viewer and the water constantly shifts between a close-up view looking at the detail of small water ripples and a longer shot moving into the distance as one's eye glances across the water.

Technique

Wood engraving is a **relief** printing technique where the image is printed from a raised surface. The design is cut with a knife or gouge from the **end grain** of a wood block. The wood grain of end grain blocks has no single direction, so the block can be cut freely in any direction to produce fine and intricate detail.

The density and layering effects in *Ocean Surfaces 2000* are achieved through the sharp contrast of white lines against a black field. The hardness of the wood Celmins has used allows her to work in tiny detail to capture the liquid, grey texture of the water's surface.

Vija Celmins (left) signing an edition of completed prints at the Gemini G.E.L. print workshop in Los Angeles, USA.

At home in nature

Celmins sharply observes the natural world, whether it is starry night skies, the rhythmic swell of the ocean, sand grains in the desert or the fragile silky threads of spider webs. Although her works look simple, they draw in viewers as the visual layers in her pictures unfold.

> *... aside from art, nature is one of the most amazing and comforting things to me.* VIJA CELMINS

PETER DOIG

Peter Doig is a printmaker and painter who is famous for his atmospheric landscapes. He was born in Edinburgh, Scotland, in 1959, but his parents soon moved to Trinidad for a short time before settling in Canada. In 1979, Doig returned to Britain and, after completing his Foundation studies at the Wimbledon School of Art, he enrolled at St Martin's School of Art in 1980. Doig returned to his studies after time spent painting theatre scenery and in 1990 completed a Master of Arts degree at the Chelsea School of Art. Since then he has won many awards, but the Whitechapel Art Gallery's 'Whitechapel Artist Award' of 1991 gained him his first public recognition. Doig has participated in many group and solo exhibitions in Britain, Europe and North America.

Influences

Doig has been described as a Scottish–Canadian–English artist. His work really reflects two cultures – his themes speak of North America while the treatment of his images shows influences of his training in London.

Doig's works are obviously nostalgic and can easily be labelled as **kitsch**. However, looking deeper into his work, it becomes apparent that Doig deliberately uses both popular **mass media** reproductions and fine art references as his source material. He does not avoid the secret attraction we all share for 'chocolate box' sunsets and picturesque landscapes. Doig embraces these images and, together with experiences, emotions and photographs of his own childhood in North America, he presents us with 'sample' landscapes that refer to these stereotype landscapes.

Doig has been influenced by his childhood experiences of the Canadian landscape. His art has also taken on a broad range of subjects while exploring the theme of people's relationship with their environment. The artist captures 'versions' of landscapes, almost as if they are variations of existing landscape we are all familiar with. He uses a loose, pictorial technique rather similar to **Post-Impressionists** such as Pierre Bonnard, whose **figurative** works include flat **abstract** areas of paint. Doig's work shares similarities with the contemporary German photographer Andreas Gursky (b. 1955) who portrays modern leisure activities.

> I often paint scenes with snow because snow somehow has this effect of drawing you inwards and is frequently used to suggest **introspection** and nostalgia and make-believe. PETER DOIG

Echoes of unease

Many of Doig's landscapes reflect upon places or events he has seen, knows well or imagines. As much as he is influenced by nature, he also responds to pop music, photography, video and the cinema. The climax in the closing scene from the 1980 film *Friday the 13th*, a mystery horror thriller, forms the basis of Doig's 1998 painting and subsequent print series entitled, *Echo Lake*. In the print *Echo Lake* (2000) Doig portrays a sketchily drawn policeman who stands at the water's edge looking as if something horrifying has just disappeared into the stormy water.

Echo Lake *(2000). Aquatint on paper. In this print, the stillness of the painted lake is replaced by choppy water and dark creepy shadows snaking across the surface.*

[no title] from the Ten Etchings series

Doig shows a preoccupation with the landscape that reveals both his own memories of his Canadian childhood as well as the Canadian peoples' attachment to the land. His own leisure interests are also connected to the outdoors and in the series *Ten Etchings* (1996) various snow scenes are featured. This series, Doig's first venture into printmaking, seems restrained. This could be due to the black and white colouring of the prints. Included in the series is the work *[no title]*. Here the artist skilfully uses both aquatint (see page 19) and **etching** techniques to suggest the mountain landscape. The whiteness of the paper in the etching is sharply highlighted by a trail of black skiers zigzagging across the surface.

Doig does not attempt to hide the emptiness of the landscape, but has ensured an interesting balance between black aquatinted shapes and blank background across the whole **composition**. The small abstract shapes in the landscape depict marked ski slopes, tree clumps and the various activities of the skiers. When looking at the small black, darkly aquatinted shapes, a range of activity is revealed. Even the puffiness of the ski suits becomes apparent. In this way, Doig engages viewers in a visual game, asking them to identify each activity in the cold, snowy environment.

Some of the other works in the *Ten Etchings* series continue the theme of snow-clad landscapes, but also include images of Doig's typical, mysterious views through trees. These tree vistas allow glimpses of buildings with no visible inhabitants, or portray people captured in a quiet, isolated world.

Doig produced this work by etching black outlines on a metal plate and filling in shades of tone using the aquatint technique. In [*no title*], he uses the aquatint technique to create flat, abstract shapes with none of the variation in tone that he uses for instance in *Echo Lake* pictured on page 17. Yet, he manages to compose a mountain scene by carefully placing black, outline shapes onto the white background of the paper. By using a small amount of black, Doig has also managed to conjure the whiteness of the snow, the crisp freshness of the mountain climate and a sense of space – even though this work is on a small scale. Quite magically the slope and activities become alive on the paper.

Aquatint

Aquatint is a method used to produce tonal areas rather than lines. A metal **plate** is covered with grains of rosin, a type of resin, and heated to stick to the surface. The plate is then immersed in a liquid acid solution. The acid eats the metal around the rosin grains and produces small circles that hold ink for printing. Artists can control the darkness of the aquatint by immersing the plate for longer in the acid solution. The area of the aquatint can be controlled by protecting certain parts of the plate from the acid.

My work is about other worlds, geographically and mentally.
PETER DOIG

RICHARD HAMILTON

Richard Hamilton's unique work shows a curiosity for using unusual techniques and methods. He was born in London, UK, in 1922. He studied **draughtsmanship** and worked as a tool designer, and then attended the Slade School of Art. He helped form the 'Independent Group' of artists and writers at the Institute of Contemporary Arts in the 1950s. Here his interest in **Pop Art** developed on the basis that: 'all art is equal whether you are Elvis Presley or Picasso'.

A range of techniques

Hamilton's work as a printmaker combines a range of techniques, which include **engraving**, **etching** and **screenprint**. His images are often digitally altered on the computer and his involvement with print technology has made him one of the leading artists in modern printmaking. He began creating computer-generated works in the 1980s using the software Quantel Desktop Paintbox®. His work is in many public collections throughout the world, including the Scottish National Gallery of Modern Art in Edinburgh, the Fitzwilliam Museum in Cambridge, the British Council, the Tate Gallery in London and the Guggenheim in New York.

Influences

Hamilton lived through the hardships of World War II and then saw a rapid turnabout take place in the USA. Goods that were seen as a luxury before the war, like the vacuum cleaner and fridge, suddenly became affordable to the average person. Hamilton observed this change in popular culture and was influenced by the new images appearing in advertisements. He became one of the leaders of Pop Art in Britain alongside David Hockney (b. 1937) and Eduardo Paolozzi (b. 1924), and was a follower of Marcel Duchamp (see page 7) who used everyday objects in a way that influenced many of the Pop Artists. In 1963 Hamilton visited the USA and came into contact with other Pop Artists like Claes Oldenburg (b. 1929), Robert Rauschenberg (b. 1925) and Andy Warhol (see pages 40–43).

Portrait of Dieter Roth

The subject of this work, Dieter Roth, was a painter, sculptor, collage-maker and printmaker who used everything from chocolate to rabbit droppings to make powerful works of art – he sometimes even drew simultaneously with both hands.

Roth produced a poem and etching called, *My Eye is My Mouth*, based on his idea that the mouth and eye must be fused so that thinking and speaking come from the same source of creativity. In *Portrait of Dieter Roth* (1998), an Iris print made from a digitally altered photograph, Hamilton has captured the energy radiating out of this artist. Ghosting around the face, together with the yellow halo and the brilliant streak of yellow, suggest an aura of light coming out of Roth, while the manipulation of his eyes with their almost laser-beam energy, suggests an unnerving undertone. Using these techniques, Hamilton has produced a portrait which has an energy that both magnetically draws us towards the man, but at the same time disturbs and repels us.

Technique

Dieter Roth's image was taken from a photograph made in the late 1970s for a group exhibition called *Interfaces*. After scanning the photograph into his computer, Hamilton used Quantel Paintbox® to change and blur the image digitally. In a way, the computer became his paintbrush. However he was not happy with the actual printed output. Alongside a number of other ideas, the image lay waiting for computer print technology to catch up and new inks to be produced that would not fade. *Portrait of Dieter Roth* was finally produced in 1998 as an Iris print. An Iris print is a form of printing that was developed in 1987 when the first Iris Inkjet printer was produced. The Iris Inkjet spits out microscopic drops of overlapping cyan, magenta, yellow and black (CMYK) ink through minute, separate nozzles. A typical Iris print is made up of billions of these individual drops of ink. The result is an amazingly rich and intensely coloured print that does not fade. The development of this technology enabled Hamilton finally to achieve the right quality for this work.

Breaking boundaries

In the 1950s, like his fellow artist Paolozzi, Hamilton made collages from advertisements in magazines and newspapers. His famous collage called *Just what is it that makes today's homes so different, so appealing?* was of a room. It was a poster for an exhibition held in London in 1956, which presented images of the post-war era, like the vacuum cleaner, the TV and the comic book. In 1964, Hamilton took a black and white photograph of his original collage and added colour to this by screenprinting Ben Day dots (dots originally used to print colour in comics) on top. He developed this image into a series called *Interior*, which showed variations of the same room. Later in the 1990s, he used a photograph of the same collage again, but this time changed the image digitally. This continual experimentation is typical of Hamilton's style.

> *A **medium** need not sit in isolated purity. It has always been my contention [argument] that the first objective is to achieve a compelling image ... As time goes by I become increasingly aware of the irrelevance of making a distinction between one medium and another, or one process and another, or even one style and another.*
> RICHARD HAMILTON

Interior *(1964) is a screenprint of an earlier collage using eight different stencils. It shows various styles of furniture, paintings and pattern as well as a pose of the 'perfect' 1960s woman, in order to reflect the culture of that era.* Interior *was part of a series of screenprints by the same name, all slightly different, and all based on the original collage called* Just what is it that makes today's home so different, so appealing?

By creating images taken from so many sources and combining so many processes, Hamilton uses every available printmaking opportunity to get the most out of the final print. His work shows his originality as a printmaker who is unafraid to test new technology.

WILLIAM KENTRIDGE

William Kentridge is a well-known printmaker, film animator and **draughtsman**. He was born in 1955 in Johannesburg, South Africa, where he continues to live and work. Kentridge studied Politics and African Studies, after which he attended the Johannesburg Art Foundation and from 1981 to 1982 studied Mime and Theatre at the École Jacques Lecoq in Paris. Upon his return to South Africa he worked in the film industry. Kentridge started to draw again in 1985. His first animated film, *Johannesburg, 2nd Greatest City after Paris*, was completed in 1989. Since then Kentridge has established a worldwide reputation for his animated films produced from charcoal drawings. He has participated in major exhibitions in the USA, Europe and China, and the Serpentine Gallery, London, held a survey exhibition for him (an exhibition focusing on a period or aspect of an artist's work) in 1999. Kentridge has recently worked on a series of **intaglio** prints in Johannesburg with the New York master printmaker Randy Hemminghaus (b. 1957).

The artist and the city

Kentridge's artistic output is varied, but he uses the same creative source for all his work – his life and the city of Johannesburg. The artist disliked the dry barrenness of the Johannesburg city landscape until he started drawing it. He saw his drawings of the city almost as a form of revenge against its nothingness. His works are autobiographical and he sees himself and his characters as captives in the city. Kentridge has never been able to escape Johannesburg and he states that his works are 'rooted in this desperate provincial city'.

Brought up in a family of liberal, politically-involved lawyers, the young Kentridge was more aware of the inequalities of the **apartheid** society in which he grew up than most of his age group. The need for change was impressed upon him. When Nelson Mandela, who was imprisoned for his opposition to the system, was set free and apartheid was dismantled, he felt his childhood hopes for a free society came true.

I have never tried to make illustrations of apartheid, but the drawings and films are certainly spawned by and feed off the brutalized society left in its wake. I am interested in a political art, that is to say an art of ambiguity, contradiction, uncompleted gestures, and certain endings; an art (and a politics) in which optimism is kept in check and nihilism [pessimism] at bay. WILLIAM KENTRIDGE

Dreams in film and print

In *Staying Home* (1999), an **etching** from the series *Sleeping on Glass*, there is a connection between animation and print. The film *Sleeping on Glass*, like some of Kentridge's other works, started with a dream. The series incorporates elements of collage as part of the **composition**. Kentridge used old pages from study notes and a structural engineering handbook onto which he printed these intaglio images. The yellowing pages were first neutralised with chemicals to remove excess acid before being laminated on to etching paper. After this, small details and colour were added to the works by hand. In *Staying Home* a row of trees in planters separate the foreground from the trees in the distant background. The nostalgic title *Staying Home* and the trees rooted in soil, contrast with the moveable, potted plants with their artificial, clipped shapes.

Staying Home *(1999), an etching on paper with collage, is based on a drawing Kentridge made in Italy.*

Other influences

Mhlaba Dumile-Feni, an important African sculptor and draughtsman, influenced Kentridge's art. Dumile-Feni made large-scale charcoal drawings that prompted Kentridge to explore the **medium**. Although Kentridge's works are steeped in South African events, he also draws upon European influences. Opera, writers such as Buechner and Goethe, and artists such as George Grosz (1893–1959), Francisco de Goya (1746–1828) and William Hogarth (1697–1764) all play parts in his art making. In fact, Kentridge's drawing style can be compared to early 20th century Berlin **Dadaists** and German **Expressionists**.

General

Although drawing is central to Kentridge's work, he has incorporated and extended it in his animated films and printmaking. *General* (1993–98) is a drypoint etching (where an image is drawn on a **plate** using a sharp needle without the use of acid) printed on hand-painted paper.

General relates to the theatre production *Woyzek on the Highveld* (1992). The story is of a simple soldier who, betrayed by his loved one, stabs her in a fit of jealousy. Kentridge puts this story in a South African context and explores the economic, personal and social pressures that push ordinary people towards violence.

Approach

Kentridge considers this to be a monoprint (where only one print is produced) because the background colour on each sheet is hand painted. It is a 'drypoint' drawn on an acrylic sheet and printed onto paper previously painted in yellow. In the drypoint technique, the burr, or ridge, created by the drawn marks holds an amount of ink which prints as a soft line, especially where lines criss-cross. In *General*, Kentridge uses this blurriness to express the soft flabbiness of the General's facial features. The expressive areas around the eyes, the mouth and the skin folds add to the bleak and sad quality of the portrait. The General's eye staring though the monocle, and the medals on his chest, draw questions from the viewer. Has the General been decorated for being a good soldier, or can only people with restricted vision see war as a solution to conflict? The outward flowing shapes of the sharp yellow paint and the splashed red strokes emphasize the dark atmosphere of this portrait.

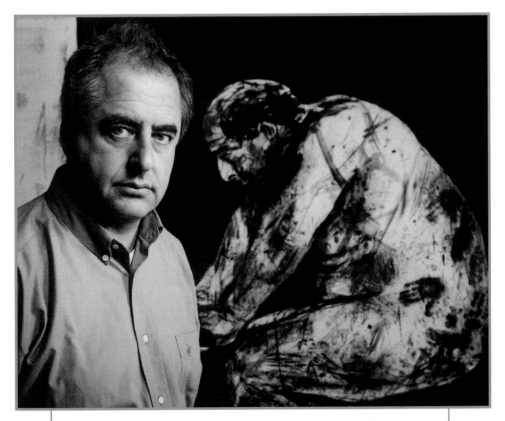

William Kentridge. He often depicts himself in his works.

ROY LICHTENSTEIN

American **Pop Artist**, painter, sculptor and **lithographer**, Roy Lichtenstein, was born in New York City, USA, in 1923. He began drawing as a hobby. After leaving school he studied briefly at the Art Students' League and then went to the School of Fine Art at Ohio State College. His study was interrupted by the outbreak of World War II. He was drafted into the army and served in Britain and Europe. After the war he returned to Ohio State College where he later lectured. In the late 1940s and 1950s he worked in **woodcut**, lithography and **etching** and began experimenting with **screenprint** in the 1960s. He died in 1997 after a long career in printmaking that was experimental and groundbreaking.

A challenge

Lichtenstein's first cartoon image was a result of his son challenging him to paint a comic book Mickey Mouse. He then started to use comic strip imagery in his work making minor changes to the original colour. He also began using images of solitary objects like washing machines, found in newspapers or Yellow Page advertisements. His first one-man show of this type of Pop Art was at the Castelli Gallery in New York. Lichtenstein's work can be seen in galleries and museums throughout the world. His *Times Square Mural* was made of porcelain enamel on steel in 1994, three years before he died. It measures a mammoth 17 metres in length and nearly 2 metres in height and is a gift from the artist to the city of New York.

Influences

Lichtenstein's earliest influences were **Cubism** and **Abstract Expressionism** and the images used by Pablo Picasso. He expanded on work already done by Pop Artists Robert Rauschenberg and Jasper Johns (b. 1930) in the USA and Richard Hamilton and Eduardo Paolozzi in Britain. Along with Andy Warhol, Lichtenstein became part of the Pop Art movement. Pop Art's aim to deal with things that were everyday fitted with his own ideas. He took ordinary objects from the supermarket and the American soda parlour such as the sandwich, the frosted glass with a paper straw wrapper, and the roasted turkey as his themes.

> *It's what people really see. We're not living in a school-of-Paris world, you know, and the things we really see in America are like this. It's McDonald's, it's not Le Corbusier [French architect/designer].*
> ROY LICHTENSTEIN

Lichtenstein's style was two-dimensional with objects and figures often enlarged many times the original size. Mass-produced posters and shopping bags printed with his images added to the idea of his art being easily accessible.

Vertical Apple *(1983). The ribbon-like strokes of colour were carefully planned by Lichtenstein.*

Brush strokes in wood

Although Lichtenstein often combined numerous print processes to produce one image, he sometimes used a single technique to copy another process. In *Vertical Apple,* he used **woodcut** to suggest enormous painted strokes. The design is extraordinarily free and fluid, as if a large paintbrush has been swept across the paper. Although clearly a woodcut, the printed surface manages to have the freshness of a quickly-painted canvas.

Woodcut

Woodcut is a process of **relief printing** made by cutting with a gouge or chisel into the grained surface of a block of wood. The raised portions left behind are inked with a roller and printed. This results in a slightly textured print that is unique to woodcut. It is not as dense as a screenprint. Woodcut is different to wood **engraving** in that in wood engraving, the wood is gouged out on the **end grain** of a block of wood. The grain of the wood in end grain is closer together. As a result the carving can be more detailed and the resulting print is finer.

Comic imagery

Much of Lichtenstein's work was based on the comic book style of using as few lines as possible to show an image. He also made use of dark outlines and enlarged Ben Day dots, which were originally used to show colour in comics. The strong black outlines and shapes are almost **abstract** and force us to look at them closely before we notice the story. Lichtenstein was fascinated not only by the style used in comics but also in the subject of comics – love, heroism and aggression. By using images of aggression in flat comic book style, he could draw on his own wartime experiences and show how easily war and violence is absorbed into popular culture. He often used speech bubbles, sometimes with the sound affects of gunfire, as in the image *CRAK!*, to add to the sharpness of the image.

Reflections on Conversation

Glass, mirror and reflection were important themes in Lichtenstein's work. *Reflections on Conversation* (1990; screenprint, lithography and woodcut on embossed plastic sheeting) is part of a series printed to look as if the images are behind a reflecting piece of glass.

The girl in *Reflections on Conversation* is one of Lichtenstein's typical willowy blondes who represent the ideal, smiling 'Hollywood' woman. The hero wears glasses and although the couple stare into each other's eyes, the meaning is uncertain. He might be starry-eyed, looking at the world through rose-tinted glasses, even blinded by love, or the glasses could be a barrier to his love. The effect of glass like a screen in front of the viewer is also a barrier. The faces appear fractured. The viewer is prevented from seeing the whole picture. The moment is close up and intimate, but we are only allowed a glimpse into their lives.

The image is a mixture of sweetness and innocence, reminding us of early Hollywood movies, but it also shows tension in the sharp shapes of the reflection across the faces. They could be whispering something extremely innocent or extremely serious. Even the title suggests uncertainty. It is a reflection on what the viewer might overhear.

Technique

Reflections on Conversation with its enlarged Ben Day dots, bright abstract blocks of colour and hard-edged black outlines, is very much in comic strip style. Although a simple image of romance, Lichtenstein has used complex combinations of techniques that include lithography, screenprint, collage, woodcut and fourteen colours, to portray it. Typically, he hides most of the evidence of his working methods, so that it is hard to see which part of the print is screenprinted, where he has used lithography and how he has achieved his colour. The Ben Day dots are overlaid to give different effects. Our eyes do most of the mixing of colour. We 'read' the brown dots against their pale cream background as flesh. Yet on closer inspection the large brown dots are not just brown but in fact flecked with red and black. The soft textures of the woodcut are difficult to see. He has also printed the work onto PVC, a type of stiff plastic sheeting and embossed it (made the surface slightly raised in places) so that the colours catch the light. As a result the shiny effect echoes the idea of glass and reflection.

JULIAN OPIE

Julian Opie depicts the modern world through a wide range of **media** that includes sculpture, vinyl and aluminium cut-outs, billboards, bumper stickers, CD designs and huge **inkjet** wallpaper images.

Born in London, UK, in 1958, Opie studied at Goldsmith's College and held his first solo show at the Lisson Gallery within a year. In 1993 he exhibited at the Hayward Gallery filling both floors with sculpture and his first paintings of *Imagine You Are Driving*. The following year he was commissioned to make his *Perimeter Wall Paintings* for the Wormwood Scrubs Prison in London. He studied further in Italy and France and travelled with solo exhibitions to Hanover, Milan, Geneva and Prague. He has exhibited in the USA as well as in Japan, India and Australia. In 2001 he held a highly successful exhibition at the Lisson Gallery in London where he designed his art catalogue to look like a mail-order brochure. He lives and works in London.

Influences

In the early 1980s, Opie was part of a group known as the 'New British Sculptors'. Subsequently he branched out from sculpture to include other media. He has been associated with artists Damien Hirst (b. 1965), Rachel Whiteread (b. 1963), and Sarah Lucas (b. 1962), all of whom produce highly individual art, but Opie's fresh style is peculiarly his own. He uses the computer to simplify everyday objects, such as cars, traffic lights, buildings, roads, people and even sheep, into pictographs like those used for signposts, or icons in computer games.

> *In computer games, simple graphics create places. A few graves become a graveyard; some castellated walls, a fortress; ten identical trees, a forest. They sit flat and need not be realistic. It is the interactive movement around them and your recognition of a classic type that brings them to life.* JULIAN OPIE

Imagine You Are Driving

Opie was commissioned in 2002 to create a gigantic wallpaper frieze as part of the arts initiative 'Tribe Art', launched by BAR Honda. To create the images, Opie drove the Silverstone track first to experience the feeling of being a racing car driver. Opie designed six huge inkjet printed wallpaper images of the racing drivers in the Honda team. Each image showed a portrait of one of the drivers alongside a view of the track.

Each print measured a vast 40 metres long and 7 metres high – in sharp contrast to the size of the bumper sticker he designed afterwards based on this work. The bumper sticker featured racing driver Jacques Villeneuve, with a central image of the track. Thousands were printed and put into *Time Out* magazine as part of a competition to win tickets to the Grand Prix. From this project came another. Opie produced a series of six Lambda prints (see page 34) based on the original Tribe Art wallpaper images. These were printed in a limited **edition**. *Imagine You Are Driving (fast)/Jacques* (2002), shown here, is part of this series.

Opie shows the track from the driver's or car's viewpoint as if on a computer screen. The simplified, flat image has a dreamlike quality, which draws the viewer into the frame. The viewer experiences a sense of freedom, both exhilarating and unsettling. As the road reels out, you expect to catch up with a competitor. It is like a computer game screen and recreates the hyper-reality of arcade games. Detail is kept to a minimum and conveys just basic information. The portrait is also minimal with its simplified black contour lines and flat solid shapes. The style resembles the way in which Opie produced the portraits of the four members of Blur for their CD, *Blur: The Best Of ...* in 2000.

Opie's approach

Opie first photographs his subjects, then uses Adobe Illustrator® software to edit the images to basic shapes and lines. By reducing the detail he highlights their individuality at the same time – showing the difference in the fall of the hair, the eyebrows, the neckline of a jumper, the body posture. The inkjet images can be printed up to any size and by designing them as wallpaper and bumper stickers, as well as in more limited editions, Opie has made his art more available to all.

Lambda print

A Lambda print is made by exposing heavy-duty photo paper using three laser beams, RGB (red, green and blue), to produce a print with a photographic quality. It is based on the same principle of printing in a traditional photo laboratory, that is exposing paper/film to light, but on a far grander scale. The image can be gigantic. Detail and colour are rich – the black velvety, the colours dense – with none of the drawbacks of inkjet since no actual ink is used. Where an inkjet printer must lay down a series of circular CMYK (cyan, magenta, yellow & black) dots of ink which overlap, a Lambda printer – shown here – blends the red, green and blue together by laser. Each **pixel** is copied at the exact colour and so produces a more exact print.

The virtual world

Opie takes on the virtual world in a playful way. His open-air **installations** juggle scale and space. In *My Aunt's Sheep* and in *Three Shy Animals,* life-size animal outlines on plastic-coated aluminium stand outside in real fields under real trees. Opie's titles in his *Imagine* series – *Imagine It Is Raining, Imagine You Are Driving, Imagine You Are Walking* – are invitations to follow the artist into another reality. We are asked to imagine houses dripping in the rain, the wet landscape passing swiftly, the swish of windscreen wipers, road spray, rain on a roof. Yet Opie's images seem to deny any possibility of rain and discomfort. The houses are neatly arranged. There are no scratches or bumps on his cars. His trees are perfect. It is as if our lives are bombarded with too much detail and Opie is giving us a simplified version.

> *I am always referring to the world, to things that seem poignant [meaningful] to me and then try to synthesize or make my version of these things.* JULIAN OPIE

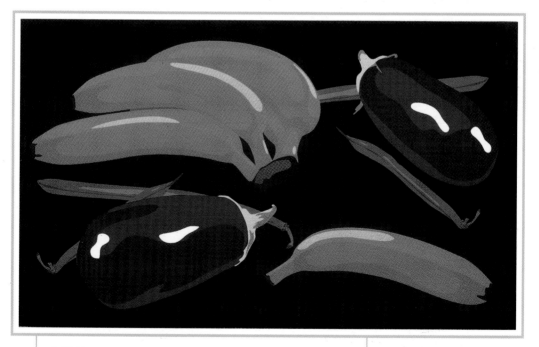

Still Life with Bananas and Aubergine *from* Eight Still Lives *(2001), Lambda print on canvas. This graphic design, with its reduction of detail, is typical of Opie.*

PAULA REGO

Paula Rego is a powerful female voice in the world of printmaking. She was born in Lisbon, Portugal in 1935. She came to London at the age of seventeen to study at the Slade School of Art where she met and married the English painter, Victor Willing. They divided their time between Portugal and England, but eventually settled in England where she lectured at the Slade. Rego's strong **figurative** work is based on a broad range of techniques that includes collage, drawing, painting and **etching**. She became the first Associate Artist at the National Gallery in London, where she painted the huge triptych (three panels) *Crivelli's Garden*, in the Sainsbury Wing Restaurant.

Influences

Rego was brought up on folk tales told by her grandmother and aunt and lived very much in her own imagination. As a child she remembers being excited by a book of etchings of dramatically lit scenes from Dante's *Inferno*, where the poet tells of his journey through the flames of Hell. Rego's own work shows the same element of moody contrast between shadow and brilliant light that is called *chiaroscuro*. The experience of living between the cultures of two countries has had enormous impact on her work. Traditionally in Portugal, men and women led fairly separate lives and the female storyteller spoke on behalf of all women. Rego's figures of women or girls, appear solid, almost peasant-like and linked to the earth. They reflect the people she saw in the Portuguese countryside and show the influence of artists like Jean Dubuffet (1901–1985) and Pablo Picasso.

Hey Diddle Diddle

In her etching of the English nursery rhyme, *Hey Diddle Diddle* (1989), Rego explores a feeling of carnival-like gaiety. Her little girl is skipping. The dog is laughing. The cat is playing the fiddle and the cow floats effortlessly against the starry sky. The moon lights up the scene in a theatrical way and the enormity of the star-strewn sky draws us into the picture. Then the sharp-curved moon directs us back to the girl. We realize she is skipping backwards on the edge of a cliff that drops into space. Suddenly the animals appear different. They appear to be crowding her. The tall muscular cat has a devilish look. We can almost hear the music getting louder and wilder as he edges her backwards. The dog has a knowing grin, the cow looks too smug, and the faceless dish darts for cover under the bushes. What at first seems a game, has turned into something more sinister and dark.

Rego's approach to etching

Rego feels most comfortable with etching as a method of printmaking. Her energetic lines, like those in the cat of *Hey Diddle Diddle*, reflect the direct way she approaches her work. She often draws on the copper **plate** without sketching first. This method echoes the way in which a child will pick up a crayon and begin to draw. If a line needs to be changed she will paste over it and draw it again.

> Drawing is essential to all Rego's work. Her advice to students is: *Just keep drawing. And keep a few secrets for yourself. Don't show everything to everybody … particularly the teachers. Keep it secret.* PAULA REGO

After drawing on the plate, Rego works with artist Paul Coldwell, who helps plan how deep the line should be etched and how dark it should be when printed.

Etching is a process where a metal plate (copper, steel or zinc) is covered with an acid resistant 'ground'. The artist draws through the ground but not into the metal, with a sharp tool. The plate is then put into acid. The acid bites into it where the metal has been exposed but not into the area covered by ground. The ground is then removed, the plate rolled with ink, and then wiped clean. Ink left behind in the etched lines on the plate, is printed on to the paper when the plate is put through a press. The longer the plate is exposed to the acid, the deeper the bite and therefore the stronger or darker the line.

The next stage is to add layers of tone. This process is called aquatint (see page 19). Parts that remain white, like the moon and area of the cow in *Hey Diddle Diddle* are blocked or 'stopped out' with wax or varnish, then the plate has rosin heated on to it to create texture. The longer the plate is dipped in acid the deeper the texture and therefore the darker the tone.

Stories without text

In her twelve etchings of *The Pendle Witches*, Rego illustrates a poem by the English poet Blake Morrison (b. 1950) about the witches who were put on trial in the town of Pendle, Lancaster, in the UK during the rule of King James I. *The Flood*, which comes from this series, shows a heavy-limbed woman crammed uncomfortably in a tub. The woman's awkwardness is shared by the viewer. This feeling of discomfort often features in Rego's work. We sense a feeling of doom. The tones of the aquatint highlight the swirling water, the stormy sky and the sharp streaks of rain. The woman makes no effort to protect herself except for a half-hearted hand over her head. Her state of undress makes her appear even more exposed to danger. There is a dreamlike quality to the chaos and strange creatures floating around her. Is this Noah's Flood? Does it suggest woman's ability to survive? Her inner strength? Or perhaps her helplessness?

The Flood *(1996), an etching from the series,* The Pendle Witches.

In her etchings, Rego allows the viewer a glimpse into scenes that appear ordinary, yet a sense of danger lurks below the surface. There is a nightmarish quality that is sinister, looming and catastrophic.

ANDY WARHOL

Andy Warhol has been considered a genius of his time. Born in Pittsburgh, Pennsylvania, USA, in 1928, Warhol's parents were Czechoslovakian immigrants. He attended the Carnegie Institute of Technology in Pittsburgh studying Design, and then moved immediately to New York and began his career as a commercial artist.

In the 1960s, Warhol produced the **screenprint** images for which he became most well known. They range from Coca Cola® bottles, Campbell Soup cans and dollar bills, to famous people like Marilyn Monroe. Based on popular culture, they reflect his fascination with images of mass consumption. His work is exhibited in galleries and museums throughout the world. The Andy Warhol Museum opened in Pittsburgh, USA, in 1994.

Pop Art and The Factory

After World War II the American way of life changed. It was the era of the vacuum cleaner, the TV, the washing machine and many other items that made life easier. The supermarket replaced the corner store. Warhol used images of everyday products like Coke® bottles and beer cans as symbols of this society. He repeated them over and over to highlight the idea of mass production and availability.

Connecting with his theme of mass production, he called his studio 'The Factory'. It was an industrial loft space in midtown Manhattan, New York City, where his screenprints, paintings, photographs and later his films, videos and *Interview* magazine, were produced. A constant stream of art dealers, celebrities, fashion designers and pop stars came and went and it became the artistic hotspot in New York.

You can be watching TV and see Coca-Cola, and you know that the President drinks Coke, Liz Taylor drinks Coke, and just think, you can drink Coke too. A Coke is a Coke and no amount of money can get you a better Coke than the one the bum on the corner is drinking. ANDY WARHOL

Superman *(1981). Screenprint on paper. Warhol loved to use images from popular culture and the* Superman *films were hugely popular in the 1970s and 1980s.*

Diamond dust, disasters and shadows

In his screenprint series *Myths*, Warhol used childhood heroes and fantasy figures and added a layer of diamond dust to reflect a child's fascination with glitter. His *Disaster* series shows brutal images inspired by press photographs. He used the image of *The Electric Chair* repeatedly as the morality of the death penalty was debated. A photograph of a shadow in his studio inspired his later screenprint series, *Shadows*. The idea of shadow is hard to grasp. It is an image of nothing and yet also something in its own right. Warhol's *Shadows* are very real. Perhaps they are the trace of his thoughts on death. He died unexpectedly after an operation in 1987 at the age of 65.

Marilyn

Warhol's images of film star Marilyn Monroe, actress Liz Taylor, president's wife Jackie Kennedy and singer Elvis Presley, express the American obsession with fame and reflect the superficiality of modern society. Warhol made the work below, *Marilyn, right hand side* in 1964.

Famous people became icons or symbols. Everything they did was written about, and their lives were made public. They were like 'products' on a supermarket shelf. Marilyn Monroe was a famous actress who was supposedly the typical beautiful blonde woman of all men's dreams. She became known as a 'pin-up' – a girl whose photograph men in the 1950s pinned up in the workplace or in their homes. After her death, Warhol made more than 20 screenprints of her, based on a photograph from the 1953 film, *Niagara*. By repeating the image again and again – known as multiples – he highlights the wide distribution of her image throughout the **mass media** of TV, film and print. She was a 'product'. In doing so he perhaps reflects what drove Monroe to end her life by taking an overdose of sleeping pills.

Focusing in on the image

By cutting the photographic image to show only Marilyn's face and emphasizing her lips, eyes and hair, Warhol created not so much a likeness but a symbol of the perfect 'pin-up'. The image focuses on the features that represented Marilyn Monroe in the public imagination: the blonde-dyed hair, the wide smile, the full lips, the sultry long-lashed eyes.

Using screenprinting effects

By using screenprint, Warhol deliberately chose a printing technique associated with commercial advertising. This accentuated the fact that Marilyn's face was a commodity or product. The images are super-charged with colour – the backgrounds bright, the eye shadow brilliant. The red of her face jumps out with such intensity that by comparison the grey or green shadows in her hair and below her cheekbones, look pale instead of dark. This gives the image the appearance of a negative where dark and light is reversed. It has a ghostlike effect. The viewer wonders if the person might disappear or fade away completely.

Warhol has purposefully overlapped, or misaligned, the different layers of stencils while screenprinting, so colours are not printed within the outline. This gives a sense of vibration around the face, which might suggest the shimmer of 'stardom' but emphasizes the idea of her not being real. The images ask the question: Do we know the real Marilyn?

Screenprint

Screenprinting is a stencil printing technique. A screen is stretched over a frame and parts are blocked out with a stencil. Ink is then dragged across the screen with a rubber squeegee. The ink passes through the areas that are not blocked off and prints onto the paper underneath. Several screens are used to achieve different colours. In modern screenprinting, photographic techniques are often used to create negative stencils from which positive images can be printed.

KIM WESTCOTT

The artist Kim Westcott is a master printmaker and painter. Westcott was born in 1968 in Melbourne, Australia. She graduated from the Victoria College of the Arts in 1989 and afterwards joined the Australian Print Workshop as an assistant. Westcott took a break from the Workshop to travel to Dimboola and the Little Desert region of Victoria in 1992. Garner Tullis, the American printmaker, invited Westcott to New York and in 1994 she worked as a master printer in his workshop. Westcott's desire to continue her work on the Australian landscape prompted her return home where she travelled to Utopia and worked with the acclaimed Aboriginal artist, Emily Kame Kngwarreye. After a spell in Mornington Peninsula, Westcott settled in West Brunswick, Melbourne, where she set up her own studio. Westcott's most recent European exhibition was at the t'Ulenest Sculpture Park in the Netherlands.

Rhythms in nature, language and music

The most important influences on Westcott's work are her personal life experiences and travels in the Australian bush. The trip to Dimboola was the first opportunity she had to work directly from the environment. The experience made her more aware of the qualities of space, colour, texture and pattern in the Australian landscape. Westcott not only uses the landscape as an inspiration, but also refers to rhythmic patterns from music and language.

Since leaving art school, Westcott has concentrated on drypoint techniques (see pages 26–27) and developed a unique visual language of her own. Her works can be seen as being both **abstract** and representational. Westcott's earlier drypoint **etchings** displayed a tight grid-like structure that has gradually softened to take on a more **organic** and irregular quality. It is possible that the Australian landscape softened the impact that New York and the influence of modernist artists such as Robert Ryman (b. 1930) had upon her work.

Kim Westcott (right) and her assistant Jo Darvell (left) in her studio in West Brunswick, Victoria, Australia.

Alad Bird

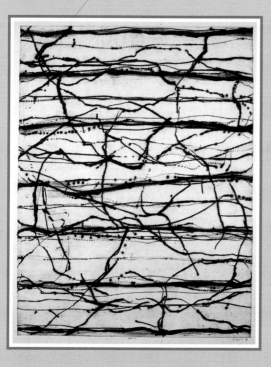

The references to natural forms in a work such as *Alad Bird* (1996; dry point on paper) are obvious, but they can also easily be seen as abstract forms. The curious linear shapes that Westcott creates are from natural objects such as weather beaten branches. In *Alad Bird* the artist has created a print using a range of drypoint marks ranging from light, delicate trails to dark, expressive lines and dots. Following the movement of the lines and dots, different landscapes and views appear in the picture through twisted branches.

> *… the tea-trees and she-oaks are affected by the harsh climatic conditions of the coastal environment, so you have these wild eccentric, twisted tree forms. I saw the branches as lines and the leaves as dots …* KIM WESTCOTT

Technique

Since 1995 Westcott has brought a new dimension to printmaking by her process of drypoint **encaustic** painting in which she combines printmaking with painting techniques. In her latest work the artist's imagery seems earthier and resembles aspects of Aboriginal art.

ADRIAN WISZNIEWSKI

Painter, **draughtsman** and printmaker, Adrian Wiszniewski was born in 1958 in Glasgow, Scotland. He studied at the Mackintosh School of Architecture and the Glasgow School of Art. He held his first solo exhibition in Glasgow and London in 1984. His printmaking techniques cover **etching**, **screenprint**, **woodcut**, **linocut** and **lithography** but his openness to experimentation has led him to ceramics, TV screenplays, flag and even carpet design. He constantly seeks projects that test and expand the way he works. He has also exhibited in Belgium, Japan and Australia and his work is in the Museum of Modern Art in New York, the Scottish National Gallery of Modern Art in Edinburgh, the Tate Gallery and the Victoria and Albert Museum in London.

Growing up in Glasgow

Adrian Wiszniewski became one of the young 'New Glasgow Boys' in the 1980s. The group included fellow Glasgow artists, Steven Campbell (b. 1953), Ken Currie (b. 1960) and Peter Howson (b. 1958). They were influenced by the German painters, Georg Baselitz (b. 1938), A. R. Penck (b. 1939), and Jörg Immendorf (b. 1945), who were known as the 'New Wild Ones' and produced large-scale sometimes violent **figurative** works. **Neo-Expressionism** is the term given to this type of art where reality is changed or distorted by the artist's own emotions.

In the 1980s Glasgow had a reputation for unemployment and a violent gang culture. The work of the New Glasgow Boys was based on the theme of 'man as a hero', in the face of this social and urban unrest. They painted in a style that was almost cartoon-like where shapes were often distorted and colours were strong. Their work has been called 'New Image'.

The influence of Henri Matisse is also strong in Wiszniewski's work. His series of 12 banners, entitled *Newleafland Flags*, painted in flat solid shapes of colour, is a tribute to the 20 stencilled images in Matisse's work, *Jazz*. This tribute is also evident in Wiszniewski's screenprint, *Interior with Violence*, based on Matisse's painting, *Interior with Violin*, as well as in his screenprint/lithograph, *Bather Four*, based on Matisse's sculpture of the same name. Wiszniewski's first linocuts were a series entitled, *For Max*, named after his son who was born in 1987.

Men in conversation

Wiszniewski's work is full of questions. It often portrays the male figure in surroundings and demands a response from the viewer. He describes his art as a conversation between the figure and his world.

His poetic-looking men have wide eyes and elongated bodies. Placed in settings which are almost dreamlike, there is a mixture of fact and witty fantasy that fools and intrigues the eye. In the woodcut, *Kunst,* which means art in German, a sculptor seems to discover his face in the wood he is carving which is Wiesniewski's playful way of suggesting he found his own self in his woodcut.

Trying to Make a Dollar shows a man in a small room with what at first appears to be a snake and another man fending it off with a pole. The snake and pole are in fact pieces of a dollar sign being made. The image seems to suggest that making a dollar is a difficult process. Wiszniewski not only plays with words and image, but also with technique. The expanse of solid colour, the sharp outlines and black textures, makes it seem as though this piece is a linocut, whereas it is in fact a screenprint, with the final black-inked screen overlaid at the end. Once again Wiszniewski has fooled and intrigued the eye.

Trying to Make a Dollar *(1991), screenprint on paper. Both men wear working clothes and are barefoot, which make them seem unprotected.*

47

For Max

For Max (1988; linocut on paper) was the result of a publisher, Charles Booth-Clibborn of Paragon Press, sending Wiszniewski a batch of lino blocks to make into an artist's book. The story tells of a man who finds a strange object in a box and sets out to discover what its use is. It has no printed text but is told entirely with pictures. Wiszniewski playfully invites the viewer to add his own storyline. A few years after completing the series he finally wrote the words of the story in a single copy of the book.

Technique

The linocuts were made without preliminary (initial) sketches. Wiszniewski drew directly on to the lino blocks with a black felt-tipped marker pen, making up the story as he went along. He completed the drawings in one afternoon and spent the next few days cutting the 25 images. Like the lines of his drawings, the grooves of his cuts appear as a single fluid motion. This gives a sense of freshness to the work. Each image is printed in a single colour. He has given the book poetic rhythm by dividing it into 3 groups of 7 colours and 1 group of 4 colours. The 7th, 14th and 21st images are printed in black to mark these divisions.

The fishing-friend uprooted the object but it was a plant! *Image 7 from the series,* For Max *(1988).*

Linocut

In linocut the artist uses a gouge (knife) to cut into a piece of linoleum (a material made up of cork mixed with linseed oil on a canvas base usually used as floor covering) to make the design. Different blades achieve different marks that can be wide or fine depending on the shape of the blade and depending how deeply the line is cut. The cut can be made to produce a single line or smaller marks made to produce texture. The lino block is then inked and printed either by passing the paper and the lino through a press or printing manually on to paper. Large areas of lino left uncut will produce large flat areas of colour. A linocut can either be in a single colour or more colours can be added by overprinting with further blocks.

The situation in my pictures is never resolved ... I'd rather paint questions than answers. That way you are not preaching you're discussing things with the viewer. ADRIAN WISZNIEWSKI

TIMELINE

Prehistory	**Engraving** first used in cave art on rocks and bones
400s	The **woodcut** is used in China to print textiles
1151	First European paper is produced in Játava, Spain
Late 1300s	The woodcut is used in Europe for textile printing
1446	Earliest dated print engraving is produced in Germany
1513	First dated **etching** is made by Swiss artist Urs Graf
Early 1600s	**Mezzotint** is developed by Ludwig von Siegen
1600s	*Ukiyo-e* school of printmaking emerges in Japan
Late 1700s	Thomas Bewick develops wood engraving technique in England
1769	Royal Academy of Art in London is founded
1798	Alois Senefelder discovers **lithography** process in Munich
1839	Frenchman Louis Daguerre (1789–1851) produces first commercially successful photographs – the daguerreotype
1879	Ben Day dots invented by Benjamin Day
1881	Pablo Picasso is born in Málaga, Spain. He is responsible for the revival of the print in the 20th century.
1912	**Cubists** begin to experiment with collage technique
1914–18	World War I
1917	Marcel Duchamp, the French **Dadaist**, exhibits 'readymades', including *Fountain*, a porcelain urinal
1922	Richard Hamilton is born in London, UK
1923	Roy Lichtenstein is born in New York, USA
1928	Andy Warhol is born in Pittsburg, USA
1929	MoMA, the first major American museum devoted to 20th century art is founded in New York.
	Stock market crashes causing the Great Depression
1934	Comic strip artist Alex Raymond creates *Flash Gordon*. Eleven-year-old Roy Lichtenstein becomes an avid fan.
	Paula Rego is born in Lisbon, Portugal
1938	Vija Celmins is born in Riga, Latvia
1939	World War II breaks out
1948	**Abstract Expressionism** starts to develop
*c.*1950	Picasso and Matisse adopt and popularise **linocut** process
1953	Elvis Presley makes his first record
1955	William Kentridge is born in Johannesburg, South Africa
1956	Richard Hamilton's collage poster, *Just what is it that makes today's homes so different, so appealing?* marks beginning of **Pop Art** movement

1957	Chila Kumari Burman is born in Liverpool, England
1958	Julian Opie is born in London, England
	Adrian Wiszniewski is born in Glasgow, Scotland
1959	Peter Doig is born in Edinburgh, Scotland
1960	Warhol starts making hand-painted pictures based on comic strips and advertisements
1961	Roy Lichtenstein paints Mickey Mouse and other comic images
1962	Warhol produces **screenprints** of Marilyn Monroe after her death. The first important exhibition of Pop Art, *The New Realists*, takes place in New York.
1967	Warhol produces the first album cover for the band *Velvet Underground*
1968	Kim Westcott is born in Melbourne, Australia
1969	Woodstock Art and Music Festival and Neil Armstrong's walk on the Moon becomes a source of inspiration for artists like Warhol and Celmins
1980	CDs appear in shops and the age of digital image manipulation begins
1983	Julian Opie's first solo show at the Lisson Gallery, London
	Peter Doig's first solo exhibition in America
1987	Warhol dies unexpectedly after an operation
1988	Adrian Wiszniewski produces *For Max* linocuts. The World Wide Web (www) is developed in Switzerland.
1992	Richard Hamilton produces computer-generated updated version of the 1956 collage *Just what is it that makes today's homes so different?* – 150,000 British radio listeners enter competition for 5000 prints
1997	Roy Lichtenstein dies
2000	Julian Opie designs CD cover, *Blur: the best of …*
	Tate Modern opens on Bankside, London, exhibiting prints alongside major paintings
2001	Peter Doig publishes *100 Years Ago 2001*, a series of eight colour etchings with The Paragon Press
2002	*Imagine You Are Driving (fast)* series of Lambda prints by Julian Opie exhibited for the first time at the Alan Cristea Gallery, London
2003	New Saatchi Gallery opens in County Hall, South Bank, London.

GLOSSARY

abstract art that does not imitate or represent physical reality, sometimes referred to as non-figurative or non-representational

Abstract Expressionism style of art that emerged in New York in the 1940s, often showing freely scribbled marks as in Jackson Pollock's work

apartheid separating people based on race or colour. A policy adopted by the South African Nationalist Government in 1948.

Cibachrome high quality photographic printing process on to plastic paper. Also known as a C-Print.

composition arrangement of elements or objects in an artwork

conceptual artwork where the idea is considered more important than the actual end product

Cubism art movement led by Picasso and Braque and begun in around 1907, in which three-dimensional facets or sides of a single object are shown on a flat surface

Dadaists group of artists who started an art movement in Zürich in 1916. They wanted to free themselves from all artistic conventions.

digital printing laser or inkjet printing where the signal to output comes from a computer

draughtsman someone who is good at the technical aspects of drawing

edition complete number of prints 'pulled' (pulled away) from the plate, stone, block or screen and numbered and signed by the artist

encaustic hot wax painting technique that combines beeswax, resin and pigments. Heat is used to blend the paint mixture and then to apply the paint on to a canvas support.

end grain woodblock cut across the grain of a tree trunk. End grain is suitable for fine detail.

engraving process of cutting into metal plates or wood with a burin. A burin is a square-shaped steel rod sliced through at a slant to make a diamond-shaped head that has a sharp point and produces a clean-edged line.

etching intaglio printing process where metal plates are covered with acid-resistant layers. A sharp tool is used to draw a design onto the plate, which is then etched in an acid solution.

Expressionism/Expressionist art movement begun in France but most popular in Germany in the early 1900s. It often showed exaggerated and distorted forms and colours. Expressionists include Wassily Kandinsky and Paul Klee.

figurative art that represents reality where recognizable figures and objects are portrayed

inkjet printing directly to paper or material from a digital file by means of a stream of fine quick-drying ink drops, controlled by the computer

installation particular way in which the artist or curator arranges artworks in an exhibition space which relies on the space as part of the effect

intaglio from the Italian word meaning 'to cut into'. It refers to printmaking processes that include etching, engraving, aquatint and mezzotint. Ink is pressed into lines cut into the surface of the plate. The pressure of the printing press enables the ink to be lifted and transferred on to paper.

introspection looking inward and thinking about your own emotional state

kitsch sentimental art which is often garish and attempts to be cute

laser print a print produced on a printer, which uses toner rather than ink to produce images through a combination of heat and laser beams

linocut relief method of printing using linoleum blocks cut with a gouge

lithography method in which the stone or plate from which the print is taken, is completely flat. The method is based upon the principle that grease repels water. An image is made in a greasy medium. The surface is then dampened with water and oily ink applied with a roller, and sticks only to the drawing.

mass media media like television, newspapers, magazines and radio that communicate with large sectors of the public

medium/media different types of material, such as paint, ink; also different types of art form, like painting, collage, printmaking

mezzotint intaglio process where the plate is roughened to make ridges and then the design is polished to make the plate smooth in places to produce a range of tones that form an image

Neo-Expressionism violent figurative (non-abstract) art where reality is distorted in the shapes as well as in the use of colour

organic natural design, development or growth as in plants or human organs

photogravure process in which a photographic image is transferred on to an etching plate

pixel minute dots that make up a solid area of colour and brightness on a digital screen. In magnified form the pixels appear as blocks.

plate copper, steel or zinc metallic plate used in intaglio printing

Pop Art movement started in the USA in the 1950s with images that were based on popular culture, such as Coke bottles

Post-Impressionism art movement after Impressionism. The main exponents were Paul Cézanne, Paul Gauguin and Vincent van Gogh. These artists explored colour, line and composition in new ways.

print-run collective result of running an image through a press at a single session

relief print print taken from the raised inked surface of a linoleum block or woodcut

screenprint method of stencil printmaking in which ink is pulled through a meshed surface stretched across a frame

still life print or painting of an immovable object, for example fruit

Surrealism type of art begun in the 1920s that was inspired by dreams and fantasies

woodcut relief print carved on the plank side of a block of wood

WHAT PAPER IS SUITABLE FOR PRINTMAKING?

Printmaking papers are usually 100 per cent rag papers made from cotton or cotton and linen mixtures. The papers are acid free so that they resist ageing. Digital fine art papers have recently been developed that retain quality over time similar to traditional papers. These digital papers must however be used in conjunction with special inks that are lightfast (do not deteriorate in the light). If used correctly, digital inks and papers should ensure a light fastness of 100–200 years.

There are many printmaking papers available from established paper manufacturers in Great Britain, France, Italy and Germany for both conventional and digital printmaking. There are also papers available from Japan and Thailand. These include mulberry papers made from *kozo*, a long rough fibre obtained from mulberry trees, and various decorated papers suited to relief printing.

FURTHER READING

These books are for advanced students but they will be useful for studying particular prints or artists:

Vija Celmins, M.E. Feldman, *Art Monthly*, 202, Dec1996/Jan1997: 32–3.

Contemporary British Art in Print, P. Elliot & C. Booth Clibborn (Edinburgh: Scottish National Gallery of Modern Art, 1995).

The Contemporary Print: from Pre-Pop to Postmodern, S. Tallman (London: Thames & Hudson, 1996).

Peter Doig: a Hunter in the Snow, P. Bonaventura, *Artefactum*, 11(53) Autumn 1994: 12–15.

Great Prints of the 20th Century: Picasso to Hockney, P. Gilmour (Aylesbury: Buckinghamshire County Museum, 1999).

William Kentridge, C. Christov-Bakargiev (Brussels: Société des Expositions du Palais des Beaux-Arts de Bruxelles, 1998).

Pop Impressions Europe/USA: Prints and Multiples from the Museum of Modern Art, W. Weitman (New York: MoMA, 1999).

Paula Rego, F. Bradley (London: Tate Publishing, 2002).

WHERE TO SEE WORKS

You can see prints by the artists in this book as well as other well-known printmakers at the following museums and galleries:

MUSEUMS AND GALLERIES
Ashmolean Museum, Oxford, UK. www.ashmol.ox.ac.uk
British Library, London, UK. www.bl.uk
British Museum, London, UK. www.thebritishmuseum.ac.uk
The Scottish National Gallery of Modern Art, Edinburgh, Scotland.
    www.nationalgalleries.org
Tate Britain, Modern, London, Liverpool & St Ives, UK. www.tate.org.uk
Victoria & Albert Museum, London, UK. www.vam.ac.uk
Art Gallery of New South Wales, Sydney, Australia. www.artgallery.nsw.gov.au
National Gallery of Australia, Canberra, Australia. www.australiaprints.gov.au

SMALLER GALLERIES
Alan Cristea Gallery, London www.alancristea.com
Lisson Gallery, London www.lissongallery.com
Marlborough Fine Art, London www.marlboroughfineart.com

WEB SITES AND LINKS

Explore these exciting web sites to see more prints made by Vija Celmins, Peter Doig, Julian Opie, Paula Rego and Adrian Wiszniewski and many other important artists:

www.advancedgraphics.co.uk – Advanced Graphics London
www.warholfoundation.org – Andy Warhol Foundation
www.australianprintworkshop.com – Australian Print Workshop
www.thecurwenstudio.co.uk – The Curwen Studio
www.edinburgh-printmakers.co.uk – Edinburgh Printmakers Workshop
www.garnertullis.com – Garner Tullis
www.nga.gov/gemini – Gemini G.E.L.
www.gpsart.co.uk – Glasgow Print Studio
www.lichtensteinfoundation.org – Lichtenstein and Beyond
www.paragonpress.co.uk – Paragon Press
www.unm.edu/~tamarind – The Tamarind Institute
www.thinkquest.org/library – ThinkQuest Internet Library
www.moma.org/whatisaprint/flash.html – What is a print?
www.wilhelm-research.com – Wilhelm Imaging Research, Inc.

INDEX